Published by
Rowan Rose Publishing

Copyright © 2014 Mark Slaney
All rights reserved

Mark Slaney has asserted his right
under the Copyright, Designs and Patents Act 1988
to be identified as the author of this work

ISBN 978-1-50242-586-7

This book is sold subject to the condition
that it shall not, by way of trade or otherwise,
be lent, resold, hired out, or otherwise
circulated without the author's prior consent
in any form of binding or cover other
than that in which it is published and without
a similar condition being imposed
on the subsequent purchaser.

Illustrations by Rachel Hayward

Pre-press production
www.ebookversions.com

TASTING NOTES

Mark Slaney

ROWAN ROSE PUBLISHING

Contents

Acknowledgements

**Foreword by the
Rt Hon Lord Steel of Aikwood KT KBE PC**

Introduction	**1**
Girls' Legs	**5**
"You cannot be serious!?"	**17**
Where Wine is Made	**23**
An Italian Romance	**25**
French Supremacy is Challenged	**29**
Welcome to the Real World	**33**
Tasting Wine	**49**
The French Prepare for Battle	**41**
Tasting Notes	**59**
France	**69**
Bordeaux	**77**
Burgundy	**95**
A Journey into the Unknown	
by Jenny and Warwick Hawker	**111**

Beaujolais	**113**
Champagne	**117**
Loire	**125**
The Rhone Valley	**139**
Wine Heretics	**147**
The Far South of France	**151**
Odfjell Vineyards *by Dan Odfjell Jr.*	**155**
A Little History	**156**
The Quest for the Perfect Vineyard	**159**
Freshness and Purity *by Andrew Gunn*	**161**
Alsace	**163**
What is the Candle For?	**167**
An Onerous Task	**171**
Jura	**185**
Off the Beaten Track	**187**

Acknowledgements

My thanks to Andrew Gunn,
Jenny and Warwick Hawker, and Dan Odfjell Jr
for their contributions to this book

Foreword

RT HON LORD STEEL OF AIKWOOD KT KBE PC

I first knew Mark Slaney as a boy in our Borders village, and I congratulate him on writing an autobiography based on wine. I share his enthusiasm for the odd bottle of Chateau Musar from Lebanon and indeed I have always preferred lesser known countries of origin to the more established ones (Argentina rather than Chile, South Africa rather than Australia). My heart sinks whenever I read the words "champagne reception" as I loathe the stuff and especially its cheaper imitators.

Given that tax on wine is now around two pounds a bottle as against 2p in France I rejoice in my annual Land Rover-load purchase of the now excellent Languedoc wines at around £5 a bottle, as I find the more expensive Bordeaux often over-rated. This is a most amusing and educative volume, best consumed along with a tipple itself.

Introduction

I have been involved in commercial wine buying for thirty years. This book is my personal view on wine. You could describe it as insider's guide on how to enjoy fine wine without paying over-inflated prices. There are wines that charge a hefty whack for reputations built on bygone days and others whose price is driven by the international super-wealthy who want to buy particular wines are they are quite prepared to pay whatever price is asked. This book offers you alternatives; fine wines at sensible prices.

Let me offer you a few suggestions, from an insider in the wine trade, for wines at a fair price that will give you pleasure and surprise your friends. Wines that will cost you less than you'd have anticipated. Some of these wines are known only to a few wine buyers and wine enthusiasts and most, because they are made in small quantities, will never reach a wide audience. These wines seldom, if ever, get a mention in the national newspaper wine columns. Their production is so small that they simply aren't interested in throwing free samples at journalists. Besides, they are made in such small quantities that there is no point in them being brought to the attention of a wider audience, as there would simply not be enough bottles to go around.

The world of wine is a two sided coin. It is a subject of romance and lyricism cloaked in arcane terminology. It is also a multi-billion pound international business. Strip it down to its basics however and it is this: fermented grapes. Done on the cheap or done to make a big business bigger, it offers you and me very little. Done with care, insight and passion however and you can un-cork something that is a pleasure to savour.

So how do I define a great wine? When I take a whiff of wine and then a mouthful, I get an initial impression and I will make a mental snap-shot of what I smell and taste. With what I call ordinary wines there will be no further discoveries or development after that. What you see is what you get. Other wines will have subtle layers of bouquet and flavour and as they are given time to breathe and open out in the glass more and more can be revealed. Rather than just tasting fruit, alcohol and tannin I feel my mouth filling with tastes and aromas that spark off memories and provoke me to actually think about what I am drinking. Whilst some basic wines seem to do no more than simply give you a pat on the head, great wines will caress. Ordinary wines after a few glasses are quite frankly boring, whereas great wines take you on a thought provoking journey; they are a sensory indulgence.

Different wines will please different palates and we all respond to different tastes. Wine writers will assign certain adjectives to certain wines in an attempt to make sense of this. Some wines are described as masculine; powerful, solid and so forth. Others are described a feminine: alluring, sensual, etc. Wine, like people, can be variously boring, reliable, pleasant, enchanting, magnificent or truly unforgettable. So whilst at one level wine is simply fermented grape juice, the finished result can range from dull as dishwater to something beyond sublime. Anyone can put paint on a brush and then put it on a canvas but only Turner can paint a Turner that stops you in your tracks.

Since the world of wine is crammed with confusing terminology I have broken a common rule to try to make life easier: I've spelt all grape varieties without a capital letter. That way if you find a word you don't recognise, if it has a capital letter it is either the name of a wine or a place; if it doesn't have a capital letter then it's a grape variety.

This book is a very personal take on wine and certainly shouldn't been seen as any sort of a reference work.

Keep this in mind: if you prefer one particular wine more than another and the one you prefer costs less than the other, that doesn't mean that you are "wrong" or haven't got a refined palate. I've tasted expensive wines that I don't like and I've tasted inexpensive wines that I'd have happily paid much more for. And the satisfaction surely comes with finding the latter?

At first glance this book may seem to be only about France, but it isn't. France was a benchmark against which every wine-maker around the world seemed to set themselves against, either consciously or unwittingly. Even now France influences the world of wine and some of its aura of greatness remains. My wine journey, spiritual if not literally, took me from France to Tasmania via the Lebanon and elsewhere. So whilst you'll see a chapter on Burgundy the wines that I explore in that chapter come not just from Burgundy but are wines from around the world made using the same grape varieties that they use in Burgundy. This book will take you on a journey around the world of wines which I've enjoyed and I hope you find it a pleasure too.

Girls' Legs

Nineteen seventy six was damned hot. It was one of those heat-wave years that come only once or twice a century. Whilst I spent the summer in my seaside town on the south coast of England wandering listlessly along the promenade and tramping the beach with my tongue hanging out, the vineyards of Europe were in danger of burning up. The school summer holiday gave me and my friends weeks of relentlessly roasting weather. I was living in a sea-side town on the south coast of England. The beach was packed and the town was bursting at the seams with holidaymakers. At the west end of the five miles of gently curving bay the beach was over-looked by gleaming white apartment towers and imposing five star hotels. The beach hut owners vied to out-do each other and the windbreaks were grand structures that encircled three generations of families in one go and looked as impressive as a medieval siege engine. In the centre of the bay queues of sweltering parents trailed from the ice cream vendors like the fronds of seaweed that sashayed in the water around the mussel covered groynes. At the east end of the beach the golden sand gave out to dunes and shingle. Here the foreign students, studying at the English language school, hung out and tanned teenage girls in micro bikinis lay for hours on beach towels seemingly asleep behind their dark sun glasses. All the girls seemed to have legs up to their arm-pits, glistening hair down to their shoulder blades and boyfriends who were always broader and taller than me and my mates. So during the long summer holiday I hung out with my school-mates and we lolled around like dogs too stupid to get out of the sun, tongues hanging out and occasionally the glimpse of those girls who opted to sun-bathe topless in quiet folds in the sand dunes just added to our sense of missing out. Seventy six was certainly damned hot.

Five years later I bought my first case of wine. Not my first bottle; I'd got into wine years earlier but for the first time I decided to by a dozen bottles of the same wine. Buying wine by the case now has the same satisfaction for me as buying a new suit and carefully opening the case of wine offers the same expectation as snipping the threads on the pockets that the suit-makers like to put there for some curious reason. Do they serve the same purpose as the tissue paper that is wrapped around some bottles of wine? Does the paper suggest something a little bit more special? Is the suit maker saying; take note of what you about to wear. It is just a little bit special.

The wine that I bought by the case was a Marques de Riscal Crianza Rioja 1976. It smelt of mushrooms, cloves and vanilla. I wondered if I chose those adjectives because I liked the bacon and mushrooms for breakfast, I liked the smell of cloves and I loved vanilla ice-cream. Perhaps my mind was just conjuring adjectives? Maybe the wine really just tasted of grapes? After all that was all it was made from. No, I decided, somehow it really did smell of mushrooms and cloves and vanilla. It tasted soft and silky. It was easy to drink and warming. At £3.46 it was, I decided, a bargain. For the next year I went mad looking for similar experiences. It was easy enough to work out that Marques de Riscal was the name of the wine-maker, Rioja was a region and 1976 was the year that the wine was made. Hunting wine turned me into a detective looking for clues. There were other wines whose names began with the title Marques, so I tried them. Some tasted good but others dull. I dug deeper and found out that some were the names of real people and others pure fantasy. Digging deeper still I found that some of prominent wine estates names in the Spanish region of Rioja were deliberate corruptions of French names. French wine-makers had, over a century ago, moved to Rioja and "Spanish-ised" their name. Carlos Serres, for example, was in truth not Carlos but a chap from France called Charles. There were also words in Spanish on the back label of the bottles that meant nothing to me. Were they significant clues or merely red herrings? I tried a handful of bottles of Rioja but nothing quite matched the Marques de Riscal until I was prepared to part with twice as much money for a bottle. Why did the 1976 wine from Marques de Riscal taste so good? Why were Frenchmen pretending to be Spaniards and why were some Marques real people and others pure fiction?

I did some more investigating. Well, there were some real Marques's for sure who made jolly good wine but the other so called Marques were inventions to make the wine sound like it had a pedigree and there was no law against this. I suppose this is like a commercial drinks manufacturer bottling whisky and labelling it as Glen Whatever. There may be no Glen Whatever and they can do that and that is an end of the subject. It is simply a brand name and if someone believes it is a wooded valley rather than a factory site in an industrial estate then that's too bad.

The explanation for Frenchmen popping up in northern Spain was rather interesting. Back in the nineteenth century a bug wiped out the vineyards of France and a handful of talented French wine-makers from Bordeaux, down in the south-west of France, de-camped over the mountains and into Spain in search of vineyard pastures new and made their homes in the region of Rioja.

It turned out that 1976 whilst pretty good wasn't the best of Rioja vintages. It was just too damned hot to make perfect wine but every good wine will go through phases in its development and the objective of wine connoisseurs is to drink good wines when they have matured to their peak of perfection. Drunk too early or too late and something is missed.

A good wine drunk at its peak will invariably taste more pleasing than even a great wine that is drunk when it is either too young or too old. By chance, I'd bought my 1976 wine in 1981 and it was approaching the zenith of development. The education came through having bought twelve bottles of the same wine. The first couple of bottles I drank within a week or so were really good. Then a few months later a bottle tasted even better. For the rest of the year every bottle was stunning but as the next couple of years went by and I drank up the last few bottles, each was slightly less fabulous than the previous.

In 1981 though it was drinking beautifully and of course as its silky fruit and supple tannins filled my mouth I thought about the summer of seventy six and those sultry foreign girls sun-bathing in the sand dunes. My wine education had begun: I was even learning the jargon: the glycerine that coated the wine glass when I swirled the wine around the glass was technically referred to as "jambes des filles": girls' legs. Watching the shapes the glycerine formed, this made perfect sense. Opinion in those days suggested that the legs were an indication of quality. The truth of the matter is simply that wines with higher alcohol will show more pronounced legs which are caused by the difference in the rate of evaporation and capillary tension between water and alcohol.

Sometimes, closing my eyes I found it easier to focus on the flavours and smells of the wine. Mushrooms, cloves, vanilla and what was that last whiff... ah yes, Ambre Solaire.

Being the son of restaurant owners and living above the shop I grew up assuming certain things were quite normal: I decided that crème de cassis made better Ribena than Ribena and as it was always to hand it became standard. Cooking a mixed grill under a salamander grill in the restaurant's kitchen before heading off to school was simply common sense and more satisfying than a bowl of Coco Pops. Extra pocket money came with helping out in the restaurant; washing up, then for more cash preparing vegetables, later training as a commis chef so that time spent jointing chickens, guinea fowl and in due course sides of beef on the bone all translated into an ever expanding Hornby railway, more ranks of Airfix soldiers and massed formations of Panzers. I leant to taste the difference between sole and plaice and Burgundy and Bordeaux before I'd done my O-levels and before I had done my A-levels I knew why Chateau Calon Segur was worth more than Chateau Phelan Segur. On days when the restaurant was closed we feasted on leftovers: fillet steak toasted sandwiches for Sunday brunch; Dover sole or duck for dinner. And a bottle of wine was always on the table.

One Sunday my dad and I came back after a morning of walking the whippet to the welcoming smell of stew. We breezed into the kitchen, dad with the Sunday papers under his arm and me with a Commando comic magazine tightly rolled into a make-shift dagger in case of ambush. We both noticed amongst the debris on the kitchen side from mum's labours an opened bottle of wine and the sunlight slanting in through the window showed the remaining wine level at about two or three inches. Dad always thought it sensible to keep a small wine rack with a dozen bottles at home. Now he glanced at the bottle, glanced at the rack, eyed the stew, looked at my mum and then stared disbelievingly at the bottle. I remember thinking it had a very plain looking label. He made a noise; a sort of faint noise that was half gulp, half choke and then another noise that I suppose was an attempt at the word "no".

So never judge a wine by its label: Chambertin Clos de Beze 1964 does not need a flashy label to proclaim it one of the greatest of Burgundies; indeed one of the greatest red wines in the world. Mum had needed something red for the stew and her logic was the plainer the label then the plainer the wine, which I suppose does have a certain logic.

I hope by the end of this book you'll know your Le Chambertin from your Gevrey Chambertin and why the former is worth so much more.

So whilst dad poured himself a large Cutty Sark to drown his sorrow, I poured myself a glass of what was left. One of my current favourite military leaders was Napoleon and taking my first mouthful of that wine I found out that I had something in common with the great Bonaparte: his favourite wine too was Chambertin.

About a week later we met up with friends at a restaurant out in the countryside: low beams, diamond leaded windows, log fires and a pretty young barmaid who, I noticed, had the same colour bra just peeping out from her open necked blouse as she did nail varnish. Funny how you notice certain things isn't it? The restaurant was called the Red Fox which struck me as a good name for a cunning Communist General who would lead crack troops on skis deep into enemy territory during a winter campaign. There were four adults and three youngsters at our table. Plates were piled high from the buffet spread and on our table was also a bottle of Chassagne Montrachet and a bottle of Gevrey Chambertin. Why, I wondered, did Gevrey Chambertin not taste a patch on Le Chambertin? I was to later learn that the answer was the same for why a Chassagne Montrachet does not taste half as good as Le Montrachet.

Amongst dad's numerous cookery books was one on wine which seemed to be all he needed: Hugh Johnson's "World Atlas of Wine". In there I found the answer that Sunday afternoon when we returned from the Cunning Communist and I was quite surprised when I nearly missed Colditz on the telly because I had got so engrossed in the book; it was addictive: there were intricate almost military styled maps of the vineyards; there were rows of wine labels photographed for easy recognition; just like those silhouette identification books on enemy planes and tanks. There were glossy colour photographs of vineyards and at the front of the book, best of all, there were the secret codes; suddenly I realised that I could crack the secret code of wine tasting and identification: it was all there just like an encryption device: vintage charts and most crucially the detailed specification of the grape varieties. Of course at the time I should have been revising for my school exams but somehow maths and most other subjects held less appeal than my addiction to military history and wargaming. Now looking at the wine charts I saw something as engrossing as learning about military history. In just the same way as the capabilities of a tank for example were dictated by the size of its armament and armour thickness so wines could be evaluated by the grape variety used, the quality of the vintage and the location of their vineyard.

I slammed the book shut: I now had two urgent objectives: first was to get to the lounge before I missed the start of Colditz on the telly and second was the purchase of a bottle of Bordeaux from 1978 because I had learnt that this was the greatest of recent vintages.

Oh, yes, I nearly forgot: the explanation for why Le Chambertin should be so much better than Gevrey-Chambertin...

The former is one small vineyard of great quality and the latter is the collection of vineyards around a village which may also hyphenate the name of the single great vineyard to their own village name. Thus the great vineyard Le Montrachet becomes hyphenated to all the vineyards around the village called Puligny and all of these vineyards become called Puligny Montrachet. All of which should be good but not as great as Le Montrachet. To add a little confusion there are also a couple of other Grand Cru vineyards next to Le Montrachet with their own names. Hugh Johnson being smart with maps shaded all the great vineyards in a dark purple, the next best vineyards in pale purple and the rest of the vineyards of Burgundy in pink.

The great book that I had found also contained a glossary of wine terms. Perhaps because all things pertaining to the love of wine seemed to stem from the French, since they regarded themselves as the greatest wine making nation on earth then all the descriptions were very much in the style of how Frenchmen (so I imagined) like to heap praise on the fairer sex as flattery, they doubtless believed, was the first step in the art of seduction. So wines, I found out were praised as voluptuous, silky, enticing, alluring and perfumed.

That autumn my focus of attention shifted from wargaming to wine. Within walking distance of where I lived were two wine shops; each part of a national high street chain. First up I tried Victoria Wine as it was closer. I suppose the reaction I got when, as a school kid, I sauntered in there one Saturday morning was not wholly unexpected.

'Yes sonny, what can I do for you?'

'Just browsing.'

'I can't sell you fags.'

'Fair enough: have you got any seventy-eight clarets?'

'Right; hop it!'

To the rescue came dad who bought all the restaurant wine from a high street wine merchant called Peter Dominic. Dad spent a bloody fortune there and had a credit account. Like me he had got the wine bug and the manager of the local branch bent over backwards to look after dad. In fact the chap was bent over looking after all his customers: never lift two wooden boxes full of claret at the same time without bending your knees, irrespective of the vintage.

There I found my seventy-eights. The manager was not on duty but another chap was and we nodded at each other in mutual recognition. I found the Bordeaux section and stared at the wine labels for five minutes.

'What's the difference between the Chateau Calon-Segur and the Chateau Phelan Segur please?'

'Two quid, son.'

'I mean,' I began as patiently I could, 'what's the difference in taste?'

The man behind the counter stared at the spotty teenager and rubbed the back of his ear. He reminded me of Roy Kinnear playing Planchet in the Three Musketeers.

'Taste?' he repeated the word as if it was new to him. Maybe it was.

'Yes.'

'Taste?'

I started to fear that this conversation could last until the next wine harvest.

'Which do you prefer?' I asked.

'The man smiled, suddenly reassured. 'Dunno: not tried either. Is it a present for your dad?'

At that moment the doorbell tinkled and another customer came in. We both gave the door a glance. Perhaps because the shop assistant had reminded me of Planchet from the Three Musketeers my first thought now was of Raquel Welch playing Constance Bonacieux.

I had seen her a few times in town; she went to the Catholic girls' school I had to walk past on the way to mine. I'd seen her playing tennis at the little public gardens that had an Victorian water tower and a pavilion where the old duffers shaded in between games of bowls. She wasn't in her school uniform now. Heeled sandals were laced up her bare ankles. Her skirt was olive green and short and her T-shirt was rather tight. She glanced at the rank of cigarettes behind the counter and licked her lips nervously then she flicked her hair and smiled at the shop assistant.

I saw a chance and lunged before I had time to consider the humiliations of failure. What I wanted to say was something along the lines of; "Hi, I'm sure you recognise me as we have often have walked past each other and I've noticed you playing tennis and I like playing tennis too so maybe you'd like a game sometime and then perhaps we could go for a stroll along the beach afterwards and watch the sun set and then we could sit on a sand dune and talk about life and..." however I realised that this was too long winded and what was needed to secure a victory was a blitzkrieg approach. However I also knew that for a Blitzkrieg campaign to be successful it had to be planned meticulously and I didn't have a clue what to say. Therefore in the second that I had to act I opted for a different strategy.

'I know that the Calon is a Grand Cru and the Phelan only a Cru Bourgeois but I was wondering which you thought was drinking better just now?'

I'd been certain when I opened my mouth the words would come out as a squeak so I had purposefully dropped my voice an octave.

The shop assistant, to whom I'd addressed the question, looked at me dumbfounded.

She glanced at me. He looked at me. He then looked at her. She looked away from me and smiled at him.

'Twenty Benson please,' she said.

I watched him serve her.

She took her change and cigarettes and turned to go, giving me a backwards glance as she left. If I'd had a thousand ships rather than fifty Panzer tanks I would have launched them all irrespective of the tide.

'What were you saying? Which one did you want one

then son?'

'I'll take both.'

He took bloody ages to wrap some tissue paper around both bottles and then put them in a bag. A poster above his head had a picture of a castle perched on a cloud and underneath the caption, "It's about as likely as a duff bottle of Hirondelle." By the time I was on the street she was gone from sight. I headed home on the twenty-one bus and showed dad the bottles.

'Nice. Very nice. Seventy-eights will be good... eventually.'

'Eventually?'

'Yeah, given another ten or so years'

I went back to the Hugh Johnson instruction manual and there I found a column of facts alongside the vintages charts that I had previously missed. H.J. had carefully noted the optimum years in which to drink each vintage. How very thoughtful of him; how very careless of me, not to have noticed that at the outset, I mused. Warnings from my English teacher rang in my head about making sure you read the whole question and fully understand it before you do anything. Well, never mind, in ten years' time dad would be all the more impressed meantime I'd have to find something that was ready now.

Good wines take time to mature and reach perfection: red wines generally take longer than whites. The greatest wines invariably take the longest to mature. A simple Bordeaux from a good vintage might take just three or four years before it is drinking nicely. A good Bordeaux Chateau from a good year might take ten years. A great Chateau from an excellent vintage could take twenty years or longer.

"You Cannot Be Serious"

Choices for drinking in the 1970s were, if not limited, at least not as mind boggling varied as they are today. The concept of cabernet sauvignon grown in China made by Frenchmen was as farfetched a notion as the idea that you could have a phone that didn't need to be plugged into an electrical socket and did not need to sit on a purpose built little table bought, from Habitat, which also had a handy shelf for the essential Yellow Pages. Chile certainly didn't get a look in and as for Argentina; well we hadn't even started the Falklands War, let alone made friends again. South Africa knocked out some stuff under a KWV label and it was pretty basic and there was a dribble of stuff from Oz. New Zealand was good for lamb but as far as I knew they didn't make wine. The notion that three decades later New Zealand wine consultants would be employed by French vineyards or that Champagne producers would be making wine in Australia was as farfetched a notion as considering that the Berlin wall would come down.

So basically it came down to France, Spain, Portugal, Germany and Italy. There was also Bulgarian cabernet sauvignon; cheap, good and popular, this staple wine was to suddenly vanish almost completely from the British high street wine shops when the Berlin Wall did come down.

Spain offered red Rioja and some oxidised whites which had been aged for years in oak barrels so that the wine looked a dubiously dark yellow. Portugal made Mateus Rosé which came in a good shaped bottle if you needed a table lamp base. My grandmother liked it but dad scoffed at it. Germany made Liebfraumilch, Niersteiner Gutes Domtal and Piesporter Michelsberg. One came in a long, thin green bottle, one in a long, thin brown bottle and the third came in one or the other but since they all tasted pretty much the same, I didn't care which came in what. All three were white wines but to my taste whilst Muscadet had the crunch of a decent Granny Smith these German wines just tasted liked sugary water in comparison to other wines.

Wines kept in cellars had to be stored by laying the bottles on their sides but these German wines were absolute buggers for lying on their sides. Two rows high and they'd start to slip floor-wards. I wondered whether that was because the people who made the wines knew that no-one would want to keep their wines. I decided that all three of these German wines were identical apart from the names and they tasted so dull I felt certain that the German wine-makers could and did make better stuff. Surely if Germany could make better tanks than anyone else surely they could do something more impressive with grapes?

I found the chapter in H.J. on Germany and fell off my chair. There was a mind blowing array of names, classifications, regions and it was all written in a secret military code to ensure that our guys at Bletchley Park would never get their heads around it. My brain fogged over. I escaped to the telly and switched it on in time to see some new Yank thrashing Nastase at Wimbledon. I wondered if the USA made wine; I'd have to check that one out. I didn't want to see Nastase lose, so I went back to H.J. and Germany.

I figured out that Liebfraumilch was the Panzer Mk I tank: basic in the extreme. Nothing but a couple of machine guns bolted onto the top of a sardine tin. I went in search of the German wines that were the equivalent of the Panther and Tiger tanks: the elite of the tank world. H.J. was very enthusiastic about fine German wine; there were loads. Perhaps a Johannisberger Erntebringer Rheingau Kabinett Landgraff Hessiches Weingut Johannisberg was what I should try? I pictured myself going into my local wine shop and asking for it: I closed the book and tried to say the name out loud. I tried three times to get it right. This was just plain stupid I decided; convinced that no-one could remember such a name. There was a roar from the crowd on the telly; I glanced up. American brat had just served a double fault at a crucial moment. "You cannot be serious?!" he ranted. The umpire in his high chair tried to ignore the screaming from below him and the crowd tittered. The English spectators had always loved to hate the arrogant Nastase but now in comparison with the petulant, loud mouthed American, he seemed as thoroughly charming and mild mannered as Basil Rathbone.

I looked back at H.J. and re-read the name again then tried one more time: "Hi, I was just wondering if you had in stock any Johannisburger Erniebringer Rheincow Bathroom Cabinet Land Gaff, hell you cannot be serious, how am I meant to remember this wine?!"

I pictured the shop assistant at Peter Dominic rolling around the floor, clutching his sides and racked by laughter: "And which vintage did sir want?"

So if Germany was going to be just plain difficult and produce fine wines with unpronounceable names it seemed inevitable that no-one over here or indeed anywhere outside of Germany was going to bother trying to buy them. So the only bastions of resistance to French world wine domination were Spain and Italy. I'd already dipped my toe into Spain with some Rioja, so I felt that I should now turn my attention to Italy. Was it possible that Italy could take on the might of France when it came to wine-making? I consulted H.J. but considering how the Italians had done in the Second World War I didn't rank their chances, although there was of course the Roman Empire.

Whilst MacEnroe and Nastase slogged it out, I read all that H.J. had to offer on Italy. From right up in the north to right down in the south the country was wine nuts: everyone and their grandmother grew grapes. They'd been treading grapes since Caesar was trampling over Gaul. They made big red wines, light red wines, white wines, sparkling wines, sweet wines, dry wines, cheap wines, posh wines. They used every style and shape of bottle known to man and when they got bored they knitted straw cardigans for the bottles to keep them cosy.

I was impressed by Italy, very impressed by Italy. Well, they made damn fast sports cars, the Romans had invented baths and roads and I now realised Italy made more wines than anyone else and to cap it all, I became convinced that the sexiest of the girls attending the language school who sunned themselves down in the sand dunes were probably Italian as well.

I determined that, for starters, I would concentrate on two wine countries: France and Italy. I would swot up on France because being the closest to where I lived on the south coast of England it would be the easiest to visit. And I would then swat up on Italy because I already had this image in my mind of a picnic in the sand dunes with a bottle of something Italian and a beautiful Italian girl at my side. Now I had my master plan I could get to work.

I trawled the pages of H.J. for suitable Italian wines to start my exploration with: of course the most important thing was to be able to say the name of the wine without stumbling. They all seemed fairly straight-forward: Barolo, Barberesco, Chianti. Maybe girls preferred whites: Frascati, Soave, Gavi. Pronouncing these was a doddle, I decided. The image of the picnic ā deux in the dunes edged closer. Of course I needed to know the story of the wine to show off my knowledge. I read through H.J. digesting facts and figures all of which were a bit boring and then I came across a story of a Bishop back in the 12th century travelling from Germany to the Vatican to see the Pope. The Bishop sent his lackey on ahead to spy out the best wines that lay along the route. At one place the scout was so excited by the wine he tried, that he wrote on the local inn's front door a sign for his master. "Est! Est!! Est!!!" Which in modern parlance I guess is something like; "Get down; this is it!" I liked the story and decided that I now had my chosen picnic wine. I wondered if it mattered what vintage I should buy and whether there was one wine grower of particular repute. I read on and was very glad that I had. The final paragraph about the wine did not make good reading: H.J. concluded that whilst this wine might have been good eight centuries ago it was now as dull as dishwater. Oh well, Frascati would have to do.

Where Wine is Made

To get grapes to ripen properly you need a decent amount of sunshine and warmth. That is basically it. If it gets too hot too frequently vines aren't going to make grapes fit for turning into wine and likewise if it doesn't get warm enough consistently you are not going to be able to grow vines to make wine either.

The Romans were big on wine as were the ancient Greeks. Roman legionaries on duty up on Hadrian's Wall were shipped wine from elsewhere in the Roman Empire to keep them going whilst they stood guard on the edge of the empire and stared out into the mist and rain and hills of Scotland. Curiously if you look at a map of the Roman Empire it encompasses all the old quality wine making regions of the then known world. Come to think of it, Napoleon Bonaparte fought tenaciously to keep hold of the countries he annexed that happened to make good wine but he let go of the ones that didn't make wine. Maybe the man who loved Chambertin had some clear priorities?

Back in the 1970s the countries of the world that bothered to make wine were, I believe, pretty similar to the countries that were making wine back in 1870, 1770 and perhaps 1670 or earlier. France, Germany, Italy, Spain, Portugal were the main countries certainly that were selling wine beyond their national borders. Hungary was making one special wine that was exported around the world to connoisseurs in the know and there were other slightly less well known countries doing their bit but that was pretty much it; at least as far as I was concerned.

Then things started to change; gradually at first and then more suddenly. First up, Australia came in on the scene. Australia had always made wines but had built their international reputation more on their sweet, late harvested wine, their port style wines and their bulk sparkling wine. I think it was Oddbins who, as a fairly new and dynamic wine shop chain, decided one day that they would take a major gamble and ship a container of mid-priced red and white wines all the way to England from Australia.

New Zealand had been making wines for quite some time but they hadn't really realised what potential they had and certainly not with one particular grape variety, namely sauvignon blanc. Grape varieties play a massive part in the style of wine and since there are hundreds of wine regions to learn I opted to learn the key grape varieties first as there are really only a few dozen that are used for most of the wine that we get to drink.

California and Chile both had a long wine-making history, if not anywhere as nearly as long as say France. France, in the twentieth century, dominated the fine wine world and perhaps rightly so. However it did begin to dawn on me that there were other countries out there making good wine and indeed there was one country that was ideally placed to knock France of its top slot and that, I decided, was Italy.

An Italian Romance

Italian restaurants were not a new thing but when somewhere different hit our sleepy seaside town, word got around. Dad determined that we had to visit. His best mate and their family were told and a date was fixed. Up until now my experience of Italian restaurants were places born of a dubious collaboration between Italian café and English chintzy living room with the seams between the two covered up with fish nets, plastic lobsters and postcards of the leaning tower of Pisa. The corridor to the loos always seemed to have framed photographs of celebrities who I hadn't heard of, the menus were always very large and typed on paper that was supposed to look like old parchment and the waiters seemed to like to polish plates in front of you which looked to me to be already polished.

What also set the waiters apart from other restaurants was the fact each one cruised the tables armed with a blunderbuss sized black pepper-mill.

The new place was seriously different. Instead of tables covered in gingham check or starched white cloths with laundry tags still safety-pinned to the corners, this place had bare wooden tables. The place was noisy but there was no background music; just a load of people talking animatedly. The place smelt of freshly baked bread and anchovies and basil. The bare white walls were just that: bare, white walls. I decided it all looked quite novel; perhaps it was going to be cool. Perhaps there wasn't going to be breaded mushrooms and melon on the menu? Then I saw the oven: a massive brick thing with flames, real flames. Young men were making pizzas for real, not frozen, not ready made, but real. There were tubs of toppings: anchovies, olives, bits of fish, pots of chopped herbs. It was awesome. I decided this place really was cool. Then we were shown to our table and the place was suddenly even cooler. There were no middle aged waiters with slicked-back hair and blunderbusses; the restaurant was staffed by smiling and friendly Italian girls. The only nod to a uniform was that all wore tight jeans and tight T-shirts and they all could have auditioned for the next Bounty Bar advert.

There was no menu except for a blackboard and instead of chicken cooked five ways, beef done six ways and veal done all the ways the chicken and beef were already done there was just one dish: pizza. Pizza with a list of names and to make life refreshing, the Italian was not subtitled. The grown-ups seemed completely un-phased. Dad's friend even talked with one waitress in Italian and thankfully he ordered for everyone, wine included. I waited to see what would turn up: bottles with labels however did not turn up, earthenware jugs appeared instead. I poured myself some white first: it was cool, dry and okay. I moved on to the red which was inky dark and dried my mouth like cold tea and tasted of stewed fruit: not very exciting. Bored with sipping the wines I just sat back and soaked up the atmosphere, more people streamed through the door and soon all the tables were occupied; the girls serving the tables remained cheerful and unflappable. The noise level rose and sitting there was the next best thing to being on holiday in a foreign country.

The pizza was truly fantastic and mine had tomatoes on it that tasted nothing like the tinned tomatoes we bought. These tasted utterly different; my grandfather grew tomatoes that tasted good but these tasted sweeter. My pizza also had cheese on it which didn't taste like the sort of cheese I knew and it had some slivers of meat that tasted a bit like smoky bacon crisps. It was divine but there was more to come. I had another mouthful of red wine as there was nothing else to drink.

The red wine after the pizza suddenly tasted completely different: the combination was perfect; the dryness of the wine countered the oily lushness of the tomato drenched pizza, and I demolished half my pizza in no time. In the interest of research I tried a glass of white with the other half: not bad, but not as good a match, I decided. I begged a slice from a fishy pizza in exchange for a slice of my smoky bacon crisps and with the white wine the fish pizza was heavenly. I suddenly wondered why we didn't always drink wine with food and I wondered what might work with beans on toast or curry? Dad made a pretty cool hot curry. He'd been in the army out east with the Ghurkhas and knew his kormas from his kukris.

The evening at the new Italian was the first of many. There was something about the atmosphere of the place that just encouraged a sort of family party atmosphere, and this was undoubtedly helped along by those earthenware jugs of wines.

French Supremecy Is Challenged

1979 was a good enough vintage for the French and for Bordeaux in particular but despite that it was the beginning of a nightmare for the wine-makers in Bordeaux.

I will not spend too long explaining what happened as it is now very old wine history and whilst it may seem a bit dull now at the time it was very exciting. I suppose it was a bit like Ferrari ruling the sports car world and then at the annual world motor-show Jaguar unveiled the E-type. The writing was on the wall when Jaguar made the XK 120 but the E-type was the car that blew all the petrol-heads away and made the guys at Ferrari realise that they had a fight on their hands.

In 1976 a chap called Stephen Spurrier organised a blind wine tasting event in Paris pitching the best of French wines against the best from California and a panel of judges was assembled most of whom were French. Spurrier was a wine enthusiast. The wines were from a mixture of vintages and it is fair to say that when youthful a lot of top notch French wines do not taste too appealing, but with time they can turn into something magnificent. On the other hand Californian wines frequently have a knack of turning on the charm from a younger age.

The tasting results suggested that California was certainly making as good wines as France and this prompted a lot of people in the wine world to sit up and take note. That said, Spurrier's tasting in Paris didn't really change the general public's perception and after a few days of fuss, the impact of this event seemed to be subsiding.

Just as there was a world motor-show there was something not dissimilar for wine and it was held in Paris and called the Wine Olympiad and was run by Gault Millau. I believe, but I may be wrong, that at the time all the judges were Frenchmen and that the wines submitted were tasted blind. In other words the judges didn't get to see the bottles from which the wines came. Anyway 1979 should have been a year just like any other with all the prizes going to all the French wines but things did not go quite according to plan. First prize was awarded to a red wine called "Black Label" and was made by someone called Torres and Torres was not French; he was Spanish. The French wine judges had not just shot themselves in the foot; they'd done the unthinkable: they had declared that the best wine in the world was not French.

Torres, it turned out, had been making wines since 1870 and they had always made decent stuff but in 1966 they had totally modernised their winery to introduce the best of the new wine-making practices that were being learned at the time. The wine that won the prize was made from mostly cabernet sauvignon grapes. The category of wine it competed in pitched it against the greatest wines from Bordeaux which also used the cabernet sauvignon grape variety as the main part of the blend of varieties in their wines. The Torres wine beat the likes of the famous Chateau Latour and Chateau Haut-Brion which were the very best of the Bordeaux wines and the Torres wine cost a heck of a lot less than the top Bordeaux wines that it beat. I suspect that evening the owner of Chateau Latour might have made a phone call to the owner of Haut-Brion and if the director of Apollo 13 made a film of the event ,the line might have been: "Haut Brion, this is Latour: Haut-Brion, we have a problem."

Torres Gran Coronas Black Label, Mas La Plana, as it is now called, made a massive impression on me: not just because it was so good but because it didn't taste like the rest of the wines Spain was making at that time and it tasted as impressive as any Bordeaux I had up to that point tasted. The first vintage I tasted of this wine was the 1977. Dad had read an article in the newspaper about the results of the Gault Millau tasting and he promptly went out and bought a bottle of the much talked about Torres wine. He invited our best friends over for dinner and put the wine on the table along with a bottle of a good Bordeaux Chateau from a good vintage. Dad's friend was a fan of Bordeaux but I remember the expression on his face when he tried the Torres wine. We drank it with our dinner and I thought to myself: this is awesome. About five years later, for fun, I arranged a tasting of eight wines, seven of which were from Bordeaux and the eighth was the Torres. It stood out like a Jensen Interceptor in a supermarket car-park. It perhaps didn't have the complex aromas of one the clarets and neither did it have the lingering after-taste of another of the clarets. However, to my mind, it just tasted sexier than all the other wines. Wondering whether I was just smitten by the story and the distinctive black label on the bottle, a few years later, I got a friend to set up a blind tasting where we tried the Torres wine at the same time as a couple of Bordeaux and also a cabernet sauvignon wine from Australia and another from the Napa valley. There were half a dozen of us at the tasting and it was snowing. I remember watching the snow through my friend's lounge window and I remember that we all agreed to score each wine as we blind tasted them. At the end all the scores were added up and then the identities of the wines were revealed. The top scoring wine was the Torres. Once again it had stood out like a Jensen in a supermarket car-park.

I recently re-tasted the Torres Mas La Plana from the 2004 vintage. Of course nowadays there are a host of winemakers making super-stunning top end wines. Just as every car manufacturer from BMW to Saab makes some special, super-fast model. That said the Jensen still looks damned good.

Welcome to the Real World

Having spent some of my weekends and some evenings working for cash in the restaurant, entering the real world was less of a culture shock for me than for some of my mates.

Initially I simply went to work for my parents full time and settled down to learning every aspect of the business easily enough. A few years flew by and then one day, as if reading my thoughts, my father brought up the subject that I had been mulling over for some time.

'You need to go and learn from elsewhere now.'

'Fair enough; sounds like a good plan.'

Working in hotels and restaurants back in the nineteen-eighties was split shifts five or six days a week, like it or lump it. Shifts were breakfast which on the rota was abbreviated "B", lunch was "L" and dinner was "D" and a BLD meant breakfast, lunch and dinner or more simply put "bloody long day".

I wrote to a smart hotel I'd been to for dinner once when I had been in Scotland on holiday and I received a letter back in a heavy envelope offering me a "working interview". I rang the hotel to arrange details as suggested and the lady who answered the phone seemed to know all about me and a week later I was there.

Friends of my parents had taken me there for dinner

when I had been on holiday with a college friend in Scotland and we had taken up an offer to use their caravan for a few days. The hotel had made quite an impression on me: the owner was tall, kilted, bearded and spoke in long sentences filled with long words. He exuded "presence" to the extent that ladies became giggling girls before him, men stood to attention, children fell silent and dogs would sit motionless not even daring to wag their tails. His hotel was on a seafront in a sleepy town in the Highlands, and was decorated in an extravagant and theatrical manner to such an extent that it made every other hotel I had been in look and feel as non-descript as an airport lounge.

At this stage, my knowledge of wines was pretty limited and most of my wine time and my money had gone on France. There were, as far as I was concerned three really important French wine regions and three slightly important regions. The big three were Bordeaux, Burgundy and Champagne.

Bordeaux is the biggest fine wine region in France and makes red wine, rosé, white wine and sweet white wine but the region is most famous for and dominated by its red wines which some people refer to as Claret. Grape varieties used for red wines are cabernet sauvignon, merlot, cabernet franc, malbec and petit verdot according to the preferences of the chateau (house where the wine is made). There are different soils across the Bordeaux region, that affect the quality of the wine and the different grape varieties work better on particular soils. For example the merlot vine is better suited to heavy, clay soil and this is the common around the villages of St Emilion and Pomerol, so it is the logical choice there. In the parts of the Bordeaux region called the Medoc and Graves the soil has more gravel. The name Graves takes its name from the gravel soil. Cabernet sauvignon vines like gravel so they are the preferred choice here. Bordeaux is a big wine region with vineyards dating back to the medieval period but the region really took off in the nineteenth century.

Burgundy I felt I knew less about than Bordeaux and I had certainly drank fewer bottles from this region. To generalise, for me, I saw Bordeaux as a region of carefully tended large vineyards, vines in neat rows, surrounding imposing houses, each quite grand. The region for me suggested orderliness and sophistication. Burgundy on the other hand conjured an image of small vineyards owned by all manner of people, the vineyards dotted around sleepy villages and men in berets picking the grapes and either selling them to someone else or perhaps making a few barrels of wine in a small cellar under their house or in the garage. I imagined that the owners of Chateaux in Bordeaux who made wine regarded it as an art form imbued with a sense of place and history. On the other hand Burgundians, I imagined, made wine so they could drink it and sell what they didn't want. Both images may have a tiny grain of truth though to be honest, at the time, I just didn't have a clue. Burgundy is a small   in the east of France not that far from the Swiss border. The vineyards have been famous for five hundred years. The red wines are made from pinot noir grapes and the white from chardonnay. It's reasonable to say that white Burgundy is probably the finest white wine region in the world and many would argue that Burgundy is also the finest red wine region in the world.

Other regions in France I had reasonable knowledge of were the Loire Valley, the Rhone Valley and Alsace. There were other regions that did not lay claim to making fine wine in any significant quantities and therefore I hadn't yet got around to finding out about them.

I had got a handle on the main factors that affected how

good a wine might be: where it came from; how it was made and what grape varieties it was made from. However I'd still not tasted enough wines at this stage to realise clearly that whilst, say, a cabernet sauvignon grape variety wine grown in Bordeaux might taste different from one made in California or Australia they all still tasted sort of vaguely familiar. When I turned up for work I suppose I already knew more about wine than most twenty year olds but I felt that my knowledge was tissue paper thin. I had learnt the basic grape varieties for each of the main regions of France and I had tasted examples of all the wines but scratch below the surface and ask me to blind taste something and I was struggling.

I was to find that my new boss knew a heck of a lot about wine and two of the wine regions that most interested him were two great wine regions of France: Bordeaux and Burgundy. So coming back to my meeting with the hotel's owner...

'There are three choices for you,' he looked down his half-moon glasses at me.

'Yes?'

'You can look after my bar, you can look after my dining room or you can be my assistant.'

I didn't feel in anyway to be qualified for any of these options.

'The latter,' he added, 'is much, much harder but will be a lot, lot easier.'

I opted for the latter.

I had imagined, as I was taking a live in job, that I would be housed in some staff accommodation; probably a dormitory affair where I'd get to bump into the waitresses on their days off as they used a communal laundry room. I was a little off the mark.

My room was in the hotel and was indeed a hotel room;

it was decorated in dark red, the double bed was draped with satin and the polished floorboards were strewn with Persian carpets. There was a massive corner bath in the room as well as a walk-in shower room with very large double sinks. There were stacks of hard-back books all about pottery, plants and ancient Greece and there were antiques everywhere as well as an enormous fern on a window sill which over looked a courtyard festooned with terracotta plants and trailing greenery.

The housekeeper who seemed very friendly was happy to answer all of my questions.

'Where do the other live-in staff stay?'

'You are the only person who lives-in.'

'Where can I do my laundry?'

'Give it to me in a bag and I will take care of it for you.'

'I suppose I should wear a white shirt and black trousers for work on Monday?'

'Your predecessor wore a morning suit during the day and dinner jacket in the evening.'

I drove to the next town along the coast which was much bigger and found a gentleman's out-fitters. All my savings from my first two years of work had gone to buy myself a car and even then the bulk of the cost was thanks to a bank loan. I hadn't reckoned on buying a dinner suit and a morning suit and I wasn't certain if I enough cash in the bank to meet the cheque which I wrote out. There was though simply no choice. It then occurred to me that my one pair of black shoes whilst satisfactory would hardly be up to the expectations of my boss. I knew I needed the shoes so I went to a shoe shop and bought a new pair. I drove back to hotel, and, tried as best I could, to relax over what was left of the weekend before I started work on Monday morning. I felt a very long way from home and I was starting to feel I had bitten off more than I could chew: I was convinced Monday would not go well.

Told to start at nine, I was in the office at eight forty-five. My boss burst through the door at ten past nine dressed from head to foot in canary yellow. A silk handkerchief was falling from his sleeve cuff and another from the chest pocket of his yellow jacket.

'Good morning to you, I trust you had a pleasing weekend? I am in desperate need of a coffee; have you breakfasted?'

'No sir.'

'Do not call me "sir", I am not titled, do not call any guests "sir" unless they are a sir. On Wednesday we have a Lord staying by the way, and you should call him "my lord" the first time you see him and thereafter just "sir" will suffice. Call people by their names, to call people sir and madam is a lazy shortcut and I cannot abide shortcuts: lazy ones that is. There is though a very good shortcut from the corner of the road between the old rectory and that vulgar new bungalow which will take you straight down onto the golf course and that is a commendable shortcut should you wish to walk, or, indeed I suppose, golf; I do not: golf, that is. Do you?'

'No I don't. Shall I get you a cup of coffee?'

'Not a cup; I prefer I take my morning coffee in a large red wine glass, black, no sugar and do, do organise something for yourself and then we shall talk.'

Mr M was then the most eccentric and flamboyant character I had encountered and he retains that position to this day. His hotel was crammed full of objet d'art, he dressed with more than a nod to the eighteenth century and his speech was more mannered than that of the Scarlet Pimpernel. He was a Francophile and an accomplished chef, though he left the kitchen in the hands of a head chef who had been with him for ever, as had his housekeeper. Mr M was passionate about wine and I am sure those many mistakes I made in my early weeks were compensated for by the genuine enthusiasm in his wine cellar which I showed.

'Do you have a preference for Bordeaux or Burgundy?' he asked me one day.

'I think perhaps Bordeaux; I have drunk more Bordeaux.'

'Which is your preferred commune?'

'Graves.'

'Have you tried Haut Brion?'

'No.'

'Your favourite Chateaux?'

'Malartic Lagraviere.'

I decided not to say that it was perhaps my favourite because I liked the label.

'But when you came for dinner you drank Gressier-Grand-Poujeaux?'

'You can remember what I drank?' I answered.

'Certainly not. I looked it up in my bills before I wrote inviting you for an interview. It's a curious little property, why did you choose it?'

'It was the first claret that my father bought me a case of.'

Mr M glanced at his watch.

'I wonder what is for staff lunch? Can you ask chef what is for staff lunch?'

I returned with the information.

'Shepherd's pie.'

'Very good. Do we have any tables booked for lunch?'

'No, we haven't.'

'Right, let us close for lunch and tell the others that staff that lunch will be served in the drawing room.'

'The drawing room?'

'Yes, why not? Set us up a table in the drawing room. Tell me, have you ever had Veuve Clicquot Champagne with shepherd's pie?'

'No, actually I can't say that I have.'

'No, neither have I, so I think we should try it.'

So that is what we did; we closed for lunch and Mr M, myself, the housekeeper, the head chef and the second chef all sat down in the drawing room and ate shepherd's pie and drank Champagne.

At the end of my first month Mr M took a large cheque book from the top middle drawer of his desk, opened it and picked up his fountain pen.

'What did we agree that I would pay you?'

'We didn't discuss it.'

He wrote out a cheque and handed it to me.

'Is that fair?'

'Yes, very, thank you.'

'Thank you.'

It felt that in one month I had learnt more than I could believe possible. I had learnt not just about preparing hotel guest bills, typing letters correctly, daily accounts, writing menus, but had been able to taste lots of new food and since all red wines were decanted, with Mr M's encouragement I had been able to get a little taste of every bottle that I decanted. The wine list was dominated by clarets from 1961, 62, 66, 67, 70, 71 and 75. Anything younger was eschewed and Mr M did not encourage people to drink the 75s as they were far too tannic.

Though I could hardly believe it, with the opportunity to taste so many Bordeaux, night after night, within months I found that I could actually smell the difference between the wines of the Medoc, where cabernet sauvignon dominated, as opposed to the wines of Pomerol or St

Emilion, where merlot played the main role.

In the drawing room amongst the many stacks of books were numerous ones on wine and during my afternoon breaks I would sit in the drawing room and read. At first I had retreated to my bedroom when I was not actually working but this action was corrected by the housekeeper.

'Mr M would expect you to use the drawing room during your afternoon breaks.'

'Oh, right, thank you.'

'Your predecessor used to.'

'Okay.'

'And at such times he would wear a lounge suit.'

'Thanks for the advice.'

I duly spent a chunk of my first month's wages on more clothes. Quite often I was so exhausted I would doze off in front of the log fire with a wine book on my lap only to be woken at five by the housekeeper who would set a tea tray beside me. Loose leaf tea, a homemade scone, homemade jam and clotted cream.

The long hours of work were hard, but the plus was that by diligently writing notes on every wine I tasted, it helped to fix the memory, and I found that similarities between wines started to surface. One was vintage: how the smell of the Bordeaux of 1971 or 1967 reminded me of walking in woods in the late autumn, whereas the 1970s bouquet bristled with rich, dark fruit smells and reminded me of the smell of a cigar box.

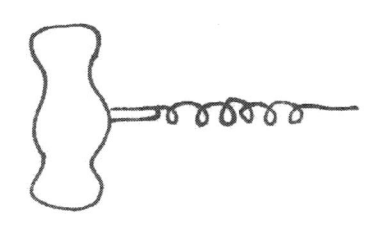

After working for nearly two months at the hotel I was starting to really struggle to wake up in the morning for breakfast duty and was grumbling to myself that the hours were knackering and that I couldn't keep them up for much longer. In the afternoon I again dozed off and when tea was brought at five it was all I could do to wake up. I headed off to my room for a shower to try to freshen up. I tipped what was left of my cold cup of tea on the fern by the window and happened to glance out into the secluded courtyard that my room overlooked. The afternoon sun filled the courtyard and lying on a sun lounger was a young woman. She was face down and wearing a bikini which she'd unfastened. She had dark brown hair, her skin was already tanned and she had long, slim legs that were a match for any I'd seen in the sand-dunes of the beach back at home. I took a cold shower and got changed for work and when I glanced out of the window again she had gone.

The next day I met my mystery neighbour. She was leaning against my desk when I walked into the office. Mr M was sticking postage stamps on envelopes.

'Ah good morning; you two have not yet met: Mark is my new assistant; Mark, this is my daughter, Venetia.'

She was wearing flip-flops, denim shorts and a baggy T-shirt with a picture of Che Guevara. Her hair was wet and smelt of apple shampoo. I shook hands and caught a whiff of perfume; it reminded me of hedgerows in spring. I suddenly realised that wine tasting was focusing my sense of smell like never before.

The truth is that most of our appraisal of a wine comes from the smell and only a little from the taste, as our palates are poorer than our noses, although in our march from caveman to modern man we have neglected our capacity to recognise a truly diverse range of smells.

There is no trick to tasting wine and the first and most

important thing when tasting a wine is to identify whether it is okay or whether there's something wrong with it.

Tasting Wine

When offered a small amount of your chosen wine by a wine waiter in a restaurant you are being given a chance to reject the wine if you think it is off. If it is simply not what you hoped for then that's hard luck. If however the wine is corked or faulty then you should decline it and either try another bottle of the same or move on to something else. Of course any decent restaurant will have a dedicated sommelier and every bottle he or she opens, they will check by smelling and tasting if necessary and if it is corked then they'll reject it and open a second of the same.

Sometimes wine will be affected by cork taint and they will smell corked; an unpleasant mouldering woody smell. Sometimes if the wine has been badly stored the cork may have shrunk, let in air and the wine will become oxidised. Sometimes the wine may just simply taste wrong perhaps because something has gone wrong during either its time in a cellar, perhaps maturing in a barrel which wasn't cleaned out properly or perhaps the wine has simply gone off the rails for some odd reason. Nowadays this happens less and the most common bug-bear is corked wine from bad corks. Hardly surprising more and more wine-makers are switching to screw-cap.

What a cork does do is allow a tiny amount of air into the wine which will modify its natural maturing and so wine-makers who make wines which need to evolve slowly and develop in the bottle may continue to bottle with corks. I enjoy the ritual of opening a bottle of wine with a corkscrew, even better still is decanting the wine; but after one Christmas when I had a bottle of Chambolle Musigny lined up for lunch, only to find that it was corked, I have always been wary of only having one good bottle of wine to hand and like to have a fall back option just in case.

Chambolle Musigny, incidentally, is a village in Burgundy. All the vineyards within the village boundary can be called Chambolle Musigny. In Burgundy the name of the village is generally very important. However the very best vineyards in Burgundy will also always be printed on the label in larger type than the name of the village. These vineyards are ranked Grand Cru. Premier Cru is a rank one below Grand Cru in Burgundy and a Premier Cru vineyard will also be named on a label. If there is no Premier Cru vineyard name on the label but the wine is still labelled Premier Cru it means that grapes from two or more different Premier Cru vineyards have been blended to make the wine. In Burgundy the name of the grower will invariably also be shown on the label. A good grower is as important a factor in quality in Burgundy as the vineyard. If the grower is not named then a negociant or a co-operative will be. The former is a business that buys grapes, or wine, from various growers and then finishes making the wine in their house style. The latter is a group of small growers who work together.

So how do you know if a wine is off? Usually, just smelling it is enough to realise that there is something wrong: usually but not always. I have sometimes quickly smelt a bottle, thought it was okay and then after a few mouthfuls realised that it is actually off. So when you are given a bottle in a restaurant to check, I would suggest, that at that point you concentrate; look at its colour first. If it is red and isn't from an old vintage then it should basically be red in colour. As red wines age they tend to go from deep purple to a pale brick red colour. Of course there are variations depending on grape variety, method of ageing and so on but as a general rule you should only expect a wine to be a paler brick red if it is old. However, classically made Rioja is aged for sometimes up to five years in oak, will always tend to be a more brick red than purple colour. Grape varieties like tempranillo tend to be paler sometimes than say a cabernet sauvignon. I'll talk about grape varieties and regional variations later: for now let us keep to the subject of tasting wine.

So if it looks okay for a red wine that is a start. Likewise most white wines should generally look pale yellow or a greeny-yellow colour. Very few white wines should look dark yellow so again this may mean trouble. Sauternes look dark yellow, but that is another story and for now let's keep to tasting wine.

The trouble with wine is it is a massive subject and can be so complex you can get stuck in a labyrinth very easily. The ultimate wine examination in the world is the M.W. and there are only a few hundred people in the world who have passed this; so that is a good indication of what a complex subject it can be. I say, can be, because it doesn't have to be complex and above all, it is to my mind always hugely enjoyable.

So after a quick look at the wines colour the proof of the pudding may well come with smelling the wine. Wine is only made from grapes and whilst the way it is made, matured and the choice of grape variety creates thousands of permutations for a smell and taste, what it shouldn't smell of is something nasty: something that when you take a whiff makes you think "vinegar", "rotten eggs", "mouldy vegetation in the compost heap" or "dead mouse in the attic".

People who write about wine for a living are I have to admit, fond of piling on the adjectives. Anyway, at the initial stage of checking to see if the wine is okay there is only one consideration: "Does the wine smell wholesome and appealing?" If it does then have a sip and if tastes good then give the wine waiter a nod and let him pour some for your partner, friend, bank manager or whoever you might be dining with.

Once you have the wine poured you can if wish lavish it with adjectives if that floats your boat or you can just say; "Heck this is good and it goes great with the duck."

I am not knocking the wine writers' use of adjectives; I have used plenty, especially when I started out, but come on, there are limits. A recent glance at just one page of a wine magazine to which I subscribe gave up the following gems; "aromas of gooseberry, guava and star fruit lead to a palate showing further tropical fruit with a saline, mineral edge." "You can really feel the sea with its salty minerality", "the pure expression of pears and apples is lifted by a brisk tang of lemon curd". For heaven's sake!

Going on to enjoy the taste of wine is another subject and I'll come to that later. I shall also talk about some of the different wine regions and styles.

The French Prepare for Battle

I became a wine geek in the 1980s. It was a heady time and a race against the clock because I felt I had so much to learn and already things were changing. First of all I needed to learn about all the wines that France produced and then I wanted to find out more about Italy and perhaps Spain and Portugal and now there was Californian wine to consider as well as Australia. New Zealand would have to wait, I told myself, besides, they were just a sideshow and the real action was surely still in the old world wine regions of Europe.

Working for Mr M had afforded me the opportunity to taste dozens of fine wines, most of which were French. I say dozens, that's not accurate: I had tasted over a hundred. I now felt pretty knowledgeable about Bordeaux and Burgundy in broad-brush terms but ask me about the fine wine estates of the Rhine in Germany and I knew nothing. Ask me about the Napa Valley or Barossa and I knew, as my father would say, four-fifths of three-quarters of seven-eighths of bugger-all.

So I took myself off the bright city lights of Edinburgh and went to work for a wine merchant.

At this point I had still convinced myself that Germany

only made loads of commercial sugary wine apart from those few estates along the Rhine and Mosel with unpronounceable names that I suspected I would have to sooner or later investigate and who I suspected made decent wine, albeit of a flowery style that I was certain would fail to satisfy my palate and could not possibly compliment any food. I had yet to conceive the notion that you could drink wine without food; for me they went hand in glove.

What had completely passed over my head was the fact that Germany made a lot of fine wine but because the British ordinary wine drinker in the 1980s had a sweet tooth, the Germans had realised that they could export all their mediocre wine to Britain and as long as it was fairly sweet and cheap, we'd buy it. There was such a demand for dull, semi-sweet German wine in Britain in the 1980s that all but the most serious and dedicated wine estates in Germany who were interested in the export market gave up concentrating on quality: volume and price were the drivers.

In previous centuries the name Liebfraumilch had been linked to a single vineyard product from the vineyard of the Liebfrauenstift Church at Worms and the charity of monks (minch) {which became corrupted to milch} shown to pilgrims by sharing their wine with thirsty travellers but in 1910 the local chamber of commerce gave a green light for wine made from all over the place and from any old grape variety to call itself Liebfraumilch and thus perhaps the first consumer brand of wine was started. The opportunity for the German wine industry to turn a quick profit was irresistible. It was like the German car industry being told that if they made rickshaws and labelled them as "Cars" then the Brits would happily pay for them.

It was a bit of shame because Germany was, and is, at heart a fine wine making country and until the latter part of the twentieth century fine German wine commanded the same prices as the finest French wine and any serious dinner was preceded by a glass of fine Mosel or Hock as an aperitif. However cheap, semi-sweet German wine caught the popular imagination and the rot set in - and it certainly wasn't noble rot! (which is something which contributes towards the creation of fine dessert wines.) It was like Saville Row tailors deciding that the future lay in polyester and the German wine export industry is still trying to dig itself out of the hole they dug decades ago.

So back in the 1980s, when I got into wine, France dominated the fine wine world and had three wine regions which to my mind formed a front rank that was still unassailable: Bordeaux, Burgundy and Champagne. They'd been making wine for hundreds of years and had refined their product and it was undeniably awesome. After these there were numerous other regions which I naively considered to be lesser, and, such was my early faith in the greatness of French wine, I considered the wines from other countries to be interesting for comparison but essentially superfluous.

There were though cracks, which even I had to acknowledge, in the plasterwork of the French wine industry: such was the reputation and price commanded by the best Burgundy quite a few wine makers in this region had become, dare I say it, lazy. In fact in bad vintages when the sun didn't shine quite enough, it was not unknown for truckloads of grapes from the far south of France where it was sunnier, or even from Tunisia, to find their way into the blending vats of the Burgundians. Red Burgundy was made from pinot noir grapes and there seemed nowhere else in the world though that could handle this fickle grape variety and create magic from the juice of those grapes, so I think a lot of people turned a blind eye to a bit of judicious blending in difficult years. White Burgundy was made from chardonnay grapes and there was plenty of up and coming competitors in the field most notably, I thought, California but for the moment no one seriously disputed the notion that the greatest dry white wine in the world made from chardonnay grapes came from Burgundy.

Bordeaux did make great sweet wine and a small amount of good dry white wine but the reputation of Bordeaux was built on its sturdy yet elegant red wines made from mostly cabernet sauvignon grapes. Merlot was also used but in parts of Bordeaux where the soil was more clay than gravel; each grape variety has its preferences. Bordeaux red was called claret and it dominated the cellars of the well-heeled British and other serious wine drinkers around the world. Bordeaux was not just a top quality region but it was large and it was efficiently organised and had been that way for over a hundred years. In 1855 all the vineyards had been carefully evaluated and ranked and every property formed part of a giant football league table which was headed by four properties. There had been one property subsequently promoted, as mentioned earlier, to join the other four in the first division but aside from that this ranking chart remained fixed year after year. It therefore seemed to me an easy job to learn the properties from the top down by name and to set about tasting them all, and that is what I duly did and it was a lot of fun.

The heart of the Bordeaux region was called the Medoc and the inner sanctum was titled the Haut Medoc. The crown jewels were the wines made by Chateaux around the villages here: St Estephe, Pauillac, St Julien and Margaux. Closer to the city of Bordeaux was the Graves region. The wines of Graves were regarded as very fine and Chateau Haut Brion was the star. Heading away north eastwards there was another area that got a mention and that was St

Emilion. This was a pretty hill-top town of old cobbled streets and like the Chateaux of the Medoc all of the wines of St Emilion had been classified although not into so many ranks. Near St Emilion it was also noted that there was another little region that did make good red wines but none of the Chateaux received any classification or rank other than having the name of their commune on their label: this was Pomerol.

In the early 1980s I discovered that you could still find and buy bottles of good Pomerol from the great vintages such as 1970 for little more than the price of three bottles of Muscadet. Today a decent Muscadet won't set you back by very much, however for the price of a bottle of the fashionable Chateau Lafleur in Pomerol you could now swap and enjoy two hundred bottles of Muscadet! That, to my mind, is bonkers!

Close behind Bordeaux, Burgundy and Champagne was another rank of serious, long established French wine regions: the Rhone valley, the Loire Valley and Alsace. The Rhone being down in the sunnier south of France tended more towards red wine rather than white: simply put black grapes which make red wine need a bit more sunshine to ripen than do green grapes for making white wine. The Loire being up in the north of France tended more towards white wine and so did Alsace over in eastern France. These three regions provided the staple wines of the daily drinking, some more special wines and plenty of inexpensive options. At the time best known from the Rhone was Chateauneuf de Pape down in the south and Hermitage and Cote Rotie up in the north of the Rhone valley. The Loire offered Muscadet from the west where this massive river headed out to sea and at the other end of its meandering course, well inland, there were Pouilly Fumé and Sancerre. There was also a lot of wines being made in between and Vouvray had a reputation for being medium rather than dry and therefore had a bit of a following amongst people who had started off on German wine and were moving towards something less sweet but not as uncompromisingly dry as most French wines.

Alsace was not very well known and was a bit of an oddity. Instead of the wine being labelled by the name of the vineyard and grower, the largest word printed on the labels of Alsace wines were that of which grape variety that was to found in the bottle. Furthermore instead of growing chardonnay and sauvignon blanc for making white wine, Alsace mostly used riesling, pinot gris, pinot blanc and gewürztraminer as well as muscat and these were to say the least a bit off the beaten track back in the early 1980s. I think a lot of people in those days didn't drink Alsace wine if they liked French wine because it was perceived to be Germanic in style and people who drank German wine didn't drink Alsace wine because it was a tad more expensive than your ubiquitous Piesporter Michelsberg. Alsace was then certainly overlooked and it is still somewhat overlooked today. A friend of mine in the 1980s who was a wine merchant told me that Alsace was the white wine that wine merchants liked to drink all the time because the quality for the modest price made it a steal.

France also knocked up some good everyday reds from areas like Minervois and Fitou and there was also Beaujolais. Beaujolais was synonymous with lovely, juicy, ripe fruity red wine that wasn't too complicated or too austere. It was very popular and Beaujolais Nouveau was a novelty that everyone went along with too. Ridiculously young red wine: freshly made and ready to glug. It was the staple of every wine bar and bistro in the country come November each year. Beaujolais is located north of the Rhone valley and south of Burgundy. The principal grape is gamay for the red wines and nearly all is Beaujolais is red. Moulin a Vent, Fleurie, St Amour, Julienas, Regnie, Brouilly, Cote de Brouilly, Morgon and Chiroubles are noteworthy villages. If their names appear on the label you're on course for a half decent bottle of wine at the very least.

Lined up against the French there were an impressive range of red wines from Spain, Italy and Portugal and now California and Australia. There were in-expensive reds from Bulgaria and some reds from Chile were making an appearance. Germany was there too with its mass market cheap sweet whites but also with all of its serious wines with unpronounceable names. Austria was close behind Germany and if you liked that style of wine there were even a few nutters, to my mind, in the south of England growing grapes and trying to make similar wine as well.

I was invited in the mid-eighties to taste the wine being made at an estate in Wales close to the English Border. The vineyard climbed up a steep hillside behind a white washed house. At first glance, with the late afternoon sun flooding the slope, I thought it looked a promising site for a vineyard. We stood beside a pond surrounded by ornaments outside the doors to a former coach house that was now crowded with washing machines, freezers, bikes, garden furniture and a giant sit on lawn mower.

'So how long have you been making wine?' I asked the owner, as he opened a bottle and poured me a glass.

'This is going to be our third year. Try this, this was from our first harvest; we're selling this locally but I can't find a wine merchant who wants to buy any.'

I took the glass and swirled the contents and inhaled. It was a faintly odd smell: like hand washed socks drying on a radiator. I swirled again and sniffed more vigorously. I remembered the smell of a pumpkin forgotten after

Halloween and then found a few weeks later on an outside window sill, the gaping eyes and mouth thick with little black flies.

'The village shop sells a lot to tourists,' said the owner, wiping his spectacles on the sleeve of his cardigan.

'Really?' I glanced up then back at the glass I held and noticed how smeary the glass was. I took a tentative sip and quickly spat the contents out. A garden gnome grinned maliciously at me from the poolside.

'Do you like it?' the owner smiled hopefully.

Paint-stripper came to mind.

'What about the last vintage?' I asked, wondering how many layers of enamel had just been taken from my teeth.

'Oh, would you like to try it?'

I approached it with the caution of a Victorian poacher walking an estate woodland peppered with man-traps.

'So were you making wine before you bought here?' I asked.

'Oh no, I was a regional manager for a sofa manufacturer. But we fancied retiring to the country, so here we are.'

I took a tentative sip and wished I hadn't.

Since the 1980s English wine making has under gone a transformation. Back then the preferred grape varieties were German hybrid cross types, and the received wisdom of the day said wine-makers in England should try to make a German style of wine and a second grade German style of wine at that. Nowadays pinot noir and chardonnay, the great French grapes of the Champagne region, are being planted. The best sites for English vineyards have been recognised as on chalk hills and slopes, where the chalk sub-strata that provides the key element to the Champagne region, dips deep underground and by happy chance re-emerges in southern England, announcing its arrival of course as the white cliffs of Dover. Global warming has helped the English wine-makers and the potential to make first rate, Champagne style, sparkling wine is now so certain that Champagne Houses themselves have been quietly buying up English farmland, with the right sub-soil.

English sparkling wine can be good and there is potential for some excellence if only the sunshine was more consistent. In time, the best English Champagne style wine-makers will be those with the courage, in my humble opinion, to only make vintage wine rather than blending vintages. By only making wine in good vintages when the weather is warm and sunny enough the wines will demonstrate quality. Just now that is perhaps only one year in three.

There were certainly plenty of wines back in the 1980s to consider, although compared with today, there were considerably less. In fact for most people then, there were far too many and it all seemed far too complicated. Some smart wine makers had therefore decided that people needed something easy to remember and something nice and simple to drink. Cue the massed produced factory wines from Paul Masson, Piat d'Or and Mateus Rosé. The former were endorsed by adverts with celebrities like Orson Wells, the middle ran a relentless advertising campaign which tried to make Piat d'Or as glamorous as the early Renault Clio adverts of their day tried to be, and Mateus, with its distinctive bottle featuring a charming property, offered a rosé for everyone who wanted to drink something a little unusual, or so they thought. However the underlying reputation of the French classics was still so powerful that Paul Masson called his bestselling dry white wine "Chablis" until the French got around to taking him to court to stop him.

Perhaps the oddest success of an international brand

was to come from Hungary; "Bull's Blood". Up and down the country on a Saturday evening in most restaurants there'd be someone un-corking the Bull's Blood as fast as you could say…Egri Bikavér.

However, wine brands aside, the bottom line was that if you claimed to be a wine connoisseur you drank French wine. Wine books in these days started with France and the bulk of the text of most books would be devoted to Bordeaux and Burgundy. Even my favourite book, which I regarded as a balanced review of the world of wines, devoted around ten pages to Burgundy but the whole of Australia received only a page and a half with the other half a page given over to New Zealand.

In the 1970s then wine brands were big business and the old names are still out there.

Be warned however; there are new wine brands lurking out there now as well but they are better camouflaged these days. Some taste pretty good and they are all carefully priced and packaged to appeal to a wide audience but keep in mind that when you buy a brand you are probably paying more for the marketing of the product than for the actual cost of growing the grapes and making the wine.

Tasting Notes

Unless you have a photographic memory I would recommend that you make tasting notes as you go. The reason is simple: the advantage of tasting wine and making notes as you go is that you can start to understand what style you like and a pattern of preference evolves. It is also fun. I liked to write not just what I thought of the wine but I note when I taste it and often with whom. Writing all this down helps to fix it in the memory and provides something interesting to look at once in a while. At the end of the day I suppose memories are all we get to take away with us.

Tasting notes can be in a fancy book with columns already created for "Colour", "Bouquet", "Body" and so on, or you can scribble them down in a notebook. This is easy enough if you are tasting wines at home but what about when you are at a restaurant or at a friend's for dinner?

Plenty of wine writers will tell you how to professionally taste and write about wine and the Wine and Spirit Education Trust who run all the internationally recognised examinations in wine up to and including the M.W. (Master of Wine) have their own system for evaluating a wine too.

When I started making tasting notes I wrote reams and it was rather flowery. Today it is simpler. My system remains much the same: the colour, the smell, the taste.

Does it taste young, ready to drink, yet to show full potential and needing more time or is it over-the-hill? Finally, when did I taste it, how much did it cost and did I like it?

Just now as I write this I have a glass of wine to hand. It is a pale pink, so pale it is very nearly white. It smells of strawberries. It tastes fruity and yet dry at same time. It makes my mouth water pleasantly. It is made from black grapes, pinot noir, the grape of red Burgundy and yet it is a rosé. Such a pale rosé in fact that it closing in on being white. It's a Richmond Plains Blanc de Noir 2010 from Nelson, New Zealand. It is certified organic and biodynamic and the back label describes it as "a delicious blend of stone-fruit and pear flavour with a concentrated, softly textured palate." Well, I don't get any smell of stone fruit or pears I just get strawberries. Is the flavour concentrated? Well, honestly how can you say? Is an Alfa Romeo fast? Sure it's faster than a Ford perhaps but slower than a Maserati. I've tasted more concentrated wines and less concentrated wines. I like the wine, it is absolutely delicious and it is also what I may describe as elegant but if I describe it is elegant I am describing it for myself. (Okay I know you are reading this but you know what I mean?) That is the problem with such tasting notes: it can just turn into waffle. "Softly textured palate". You see what I mean?

What is interesting is that in the 1980s I don't suppose there were any pinot noir grapes being grown in New Zealand and as for organic or bio-dynamic - these were terms that were largely right off the radar. Don't get me wrong, wine tasting notes can be enhanced by a liberal use of adjectives but palates are subjective. There are no stone fruit, no blackcurrants and no mown hay put into wines: it is simply our brains saying to us "Hey, you know what? This taste reminds me of such and such." I tasted a red

Crozes Hermitage ages ago with some friends. One of them said it smelt of tar and another said it smelt of kippers and a third said it smelt of truffles. The one who said it smelt of tar happened to be a civil engineer, the one who said it smelt of kippers happened to like a kipper for breakfast at the weekend and the one who said it smelt of truffles was a chap who loved to eat out in fancy French restaurants. You get my point?

The other interesting point to keep in mind about tasting wine is that your palate is sharper earlier in the day, but can be messed up by things like toothpaste, aftershave or perfume. I have been in a professional wine tasting and have seen a well-known lady wine writer promptly escorted from the room; she had come in reeking of perfume that was so strong it was going to affect everyone's nose in the room. I've been at another tasting of 1978 Grand Cru Bordeaux where because the room had been allowed to flood with sunlight and warmth during the morning all the wines were too warm and tasted pretty disappointing. Temperature is crucial. Red wines don't taste too good if they are too warm; there is a technical explanation for this which I have never bothered to learn as having tasted it first-hand I know it is fact and that is that. Likewise, white wines are frequently served too cold, and it does them no good whatsoever. However, if you like your red wines very warm or your white wines chilled, then that is how you should drink them, but please, one day just try your reds a little cooler and your whites a little less chilled and think about the resultant change in taste.

Wine tasting is an opportunity, without doubt, to show off and to impress others around you who know less. This isn't what wine is about: wine is about enjoyment and sharing. It is easy to give an impression that you know what is what but be warned it is also very easy to make a complete ass of yourself. Picture this: eight businessmen gathered around a lunch table in a restaurant's private dining room. The host is telling all the others about a new tomato. Well, thousands of tomatoes to be accurate, the ones being sold to our supermarkets. So with much smug glee, the host tells the others around the table that they have leased land on very good terms because they have very clever lawyers and the locals (in this foreign country) are a bit thick. He cheerfully announces how they have screwed down the local workforce to a very low wage and then he confides, as if he is imparting a military secret, that the tomato has been bred to present a nice shiny red skin that is actually not just resistant to being bruised when packed but it is practically bullet-proof. Better still, he announces, warming to his theme, the tomato has been bred to make it smell like a tomato. It will even, he announces with as much gravitas as a U.N. spokesperson unveiling a Middle East cease-fire agreement, ripen across a specific time frame. And on he smugly goes. Their tomato grows to a designated size very fast. It is very disease resistant. By the time the head honcho had explained all of this the lunch group were on cheese. I had got sick of listening to this, so I left others to look after them. They were drinking red Burgundy; very expensive and very old red Burgundy. They had had some seriously expensive white Burgundy first, no expense was being spared. After two bottles of the red were drunk, the guy in charge called for a third bottle. The waitress decanted the third bottle and poured some for the big cheese to taste.

"God that's not right; not a bit like the others. I'm not drinking that!"

He asked for another bottle but we had run out.

"Oh, it doesn't matter," he said, "We'll have brandies with the coffee instead."

And they did.

After they had gone I had a whiff of the third bottle, the one he had rejected. It smelt just as I would have expected it to. I poured myself some and had a taste. It tasted sublime. I picked up the decanters with the remains of the first two bottles which they had. I smelt both. Both were corked.

There's a postscript to this story. As the group of men were sat enjoying their brandies one of them asked the guy hosting the lunch who had been telling them all about this tomato that they were now selling to numerous supermarkets a question.

"What do they taste like?'

"Sorry?"

"The tomatoes: what do they taste like?"

"I've got no idea,' answered the big cheese, 'I've never tasted them."

At the beginning of this section I talked about keeping tasting notes and mentioned that it is easy enough when at home but more problematical when out for dinner or at friends for supper. When I started out tasting wines at home I made notes on those little lined cards that would fill boxes that are about three inches by five inches. Later I switched to keeping notes in my diary and more recently my partner bought me a super slim, little black book specifically designed for the job with pre-printed pages of airmail weight paper. This is ideal for carrying in a jacket pocket and solves the problem of where to write when out for dinner. Prior to this I used to scribble something on the restaurant bill as soon as I got it and my memory was fresh. Attending professional trade tastings one is invariably given a printed list of the all the wines with room to make notes under every wine. Some tastings might be of just a dozen wines but others may be of a hundred or more wines. Since

I have professionally been tasting wines as a wine buyer, the volume of wines is simply massive. A clearly kept system is imperative: I try to always taste in the late morning or early afternoon. I sniff, taste and spit each wine and jot down a few key thoughts and nowadays I will give it a score out of ten. I will do all the white wines I wish to taste before the reds and try to leave the heaviest and most tannic reds until last. I give up after around sixty wines. After that number, even if I diligently spit out and sip water between each wine I find that my palate is no longer sharp.

The earliest tasting notes I still have are from the early 1980s, then I just used to write whatever came to mind rather than worry about ticking all the boxes for colour, smell, tannin, etc.

Santenay 1973 Groffier-Leger.

"Drunk with barbecued lamb cutlets on a sweltering summer's day at lunch. Rich flavour, spicy and fairly earthy."

My wine tasting notes then steadily evolved as my palate became more educated. As I became more of a wine geek my tasting notes became more involved, self-conscious and flowery:

Chambertin 1964. Domaine Jaboulet Vercherre

"Whilst assuming a paling brown edge at the rim of the glass it still showed a good red ochre colour. First smell was a delicate mushroomy bouquet. The wine has less stuffing than a Bruck 1970 Latricieres Chambertin or a Beaune 1er Cru Teurons 1976. Very soft finish on the palate although slightly dry around the teeth and gums and suave rather than voluptuous. Unfortunately I sense a slight similarity to a bottle of Leory d'Auvenay 1976 that was beginning to age and tire. When decanting I caught a perfumed smell which was lost once in the decanter even though drunk within fifteen minutes." (26th December

1986)

Tasting notes should be a reference point to help you recall what you thought of something and as long as they make sense to you, then that is all that really matters.

Ultimately I don't think it matters what you write as long as it enables you to recall what a wine tasted and how you felt about it at the time. Looking at my tasting notes for the Santenay 1973 I can recall the BBQ, I can remember the friends who I shared the wine with and the few words that I scribbled down on the day are the mental trigger or catalyst of recall for that day, that moment and that bottle of Burgundy.

What I think is also so important is whether you like the wine rather than whether it is technically a good or great wine. The village of Santenay never makes what people regard as great wine, so I wasn't expecting anything amazing from the wine. That said; it was drinking well, it was at that same point as the 1976 Marques de Riscal had been when I tried it: spot on; neither too young nor too old. The day was warm and sunny, the BBQ nosh was bang on and the Santenay was quaffable and hearty: red Burgundy that made one feel glad to be alive on a summer's day and in good company. So although it ranks low amongst the catalogue of red Burgundy that I have drunk from the point of view of fine-ness it ranks high on the pleasure scale and enjoying fine wine should, I think, be first and last about the pleasure the wine gives.

In time my tasting notes became more objective and factual, considering colour, bouquet, taste, evaluation of quality, price, estimated plateau of maturity and where it was purchased. Filling in all of this though takes time and at tastings where large quantities of wine were presented I always feel that I'm was going to run out of time.

Now I have veered to a more succinct style when it

comes to making tasting notes. At a big tasting recently, having arrived in the morning, I calmly read through the offering of 179 different wines and decided that I certainly wished to try at least half of what was on offer. By mid-afternoon my palate was feeling pretty wrecked, despite spitting out every wine. My tasting notes for the day had started out well enough, succinct but objective. However by late afternoon I was down to writing just a couple of words alongside each wine I tried. Tasting a Nero d'Avola from Cantina Rallo in Sicily I thought the wine was really good but I couldn't evaluate it beyond that so I simply jotted down the single word: "Buy!"

I have been lucky in that I can generally remember wines, even from ages ago, whilst I struggle to remember my phone number. I suppose if one is interested then one's brain kicks in and if I'm not interested I admit that I switch off.

Tasting is very subjective and there are so many factors that can influence how much you enjoy a wine. A simple bottle of Pinot Grigio opened at the end of a long day after work when you're tired and irritable and are half distracted by the television may taste no more than okay but the very same wine from the same grower perhaps sipped outside at a street café in Italy in the sunshine three days into a well-earned holiday and accompanied by some local food could taste sublime.

A friend of mine took friends to lunch in a flash restaurant in London once. They had a lot of catching up to do and the conversation was non-stop. He glanced at the wine list, saw the name of a good red Bordeaux he knew and ordered it. They ate their meal, drank the wine and then he asked for the bill. The bill was enough for a decent luncheon for forty people never mind four and my friend nearly fainted. He had not paid attention to the vintage of the wine he had ordered and instead of it being a typical, average vintage with a few years bottle age on it was in fact a magnificent vintage with decades of maturity and had cost a fortune. This tends to prove the point that if we expect something to be amazing we will approach it with more reverence and anticipation and I think this frequently affects tasting evaluations of fine, top-end wines.

I would like to see what would happen if a bottle of a First Growth Bordeaux was slipped into a tasting of what was presented as a fifty top cabernet sauvignon wines from Chile and a panel of wine experts were told to evaluate the wines. How many tasters would be able to say: "Sorry mate, this isn't a top flight Chilean cabernet but it is actually a bottle from Bordeaux that is worth ten times as much"?

There is a great skill to tasting completely blind. One evening I went to a friend's for dinner; he was a wine merchant. We would invariably give each other bottles to taste blind. On this occasion he had a handful of friends around for dinner. As soon as I arrived I went to the kitchen to say hello to his wife and the moment her back was turned I flicked the lid on the rubbish bin, spied a bottle, flicked some rubbish off the label so I could check the vintage, closed the bin and headed into the sitting room to meet everyone.

"So Mark, what do reckon this red is?' asked my friend when dinner progressed to the main course. The decanter sat in the middle of the table and everyone looked at me.

'Well,' I swirled the glass, inhaled and then sipped and looked thoughtful. 'Obviously a Burgundy, and most likely something from the Cotes de Nuits.'

My wine-merchant friend nodded affirmatively. The sense of excitement mounted as I took a second thoughtful sip and ruminated for a moment.

'I'd be inclined to say that it is a Nuits St Georges and a Premier Cru.'

My friend looked speechless and the others looked utterly amazed.

'To me, if I was to venture a guess I should say this is from Machard de Gramont.'

'Bloody hell!' muttered my friend.

'That's amazing,' said someone else.

'Well,' I leant back in my chair and smiled affectionately at the glass I held. 'The Gramont brothers wines are pretty distinctive. They both still tread all their grapes by foot, and this wine is without doubt made be Alain.'

'How on earth…'

'Well, you see, it's quite obvious in the taste: Alain is always a little heavy on the right foot.'

France

Until the 1970s I think most people in Britain were happy to usually opt for a bottle of wine from France and a second choice was perhaps Germany, Italy or Spain.

In the 1980s there was a global flurry of expansion in wine making as demand rose. More and more people got into drinking everyday wine and so every country that could make and export wine of a reasonable quality did just that.

There was a frenzy of planting vineyards everywhere: South America, New Zealand, Russia, China, India, I think everywhere that could, got in on the wine making band wagon.

Then, rather more recently, people realised that something else was happening. Big wine drinking countries like France, Germany, Italy and Britain were all beginning to drink less wine. Perhaps it was the visit to the doctor that prompted people to cut back.

"So how much alcohol do you consume in a week?'

Europeans in their twenties and thirties had also started to swing from drinking wine to drinking beer.

Anyway we suddenly got to the point where the world was making more wine than the world wanted, so, in desperation to off load their production, the big wine producers started to cut their prices.

In the 1970s people in Britain who bought wine generally got it from a wine merchants. There was dozens if not hundreds of traditional wine merchants and little wine retailers. The supermarkets fancied a slice of the cake; well actually they fancied the cake, so they moved in. They started with offering a big choice and at good prices. Consumers began to buy not just their groceries from them but their wine. The supermarkets offered a chance to winemakers, who could supply in volume, a ready outlet and pretty soon we all had a great choice of inexpensive wines. Curiously the range of wines then declined. If you look behind the labels you will see that these are simply labels; there is frequently not a wine-maker. They are merely brands. The grapes are bought from all over the place and blended in vats that are massive beyond belief, then the wine is made by lab technicians to a formula and to a specific price. There's nothing necessarily unacceptable with that, don't get me wrong, but this sort of wine is a factory product and it has no soul. If you were to look at a picture of the Gallo winery for example you would see a factory complex stretching across a vast flat landscape; it looks like some giant chemical plant that a madman from a 007 movie might have as his base from where he is planning global domination.

To be fair to the supermarkets, a few of the wines that they sell are single vineyard or estate wines and much of the bulk brand wine that they sell is sold at a fair price for what it is, and it is okay. I have bought my share of bottles from supermarkets because unless I did I could not speak from first-hand experience.

Sadly the supermarkets knocked a lot of private wine merchants and wine shops out of business. Even many of the bigger wine merchants fell by the wayside. Thankfully though a good handful of wine merchants survived and learned to be competitive; not so much by going into a price war, but by offering service, knowledge and a range of wines that the supermarkets did not offer.

Finally, it is worth keeping in mind that most vineyards are not that big, so the amount of wine that they can make is simply too small for the likes of a supermarket to bother with. Last week I was at a wine tasting and tried a really good white wine, expensive, but good. So small is the production of the wine, the UK importer receives just sixty bottles.

Many countries and regions have wine co-operatives where grape growers can sell off their grapes and leave the wine making to someone else, albeit a collective of people. These co-op's, depending on who runs them and the local attitude and their aspiration, can make dire wine or they can make good wine, if seldom great wine. Much supermarket wine comes from wine-makers' co-operatives, and what has been good is that in recent years wine-makers have raised their game and as wine-making has got better these outfits have often pulled their socks up too.

As it became evident that there was more wine for the cheaper end of the market being produced than was now being drunk globally, many wine-makers were faced with an option. Do we keep cutting the price we want for our grapes or wine in the hopes we'll be chosen as a source for cheap grapes/wine, or do we raise our standards, make less wine but make better wine and see if we can't charge a bit more for it. This has been good news for wine drinkers because if you are prepared to pay a little bit more than the average for a bottle of wine there has never been a bigger choice of really good wines.

Anyway, to come back to the choice today of wines from France it is not so very different from the choice when I first got into wine or indeed in centuries before. However there is to my mind one key difference. France has always provided a geological landscape and climate that in places offers the opportunity to make superb wine. There are also other countries blessed with the combination of these two factors. Half a century ago, in sweepingly general terms, French wine-makers were frequently nonchalant about their business. Now after decades of witnessing their livelihood and reputation whittled away by foreign competition they are fighting back.

There are now numerous wine-makers the length and breadth of France who are striving to make the best wines possible from their particular vineyard location; there has been a renaissance in wine-making and this has not come from any one specific region but it has come from individuals in many regions who are passionate about what they do.

However whilst some wine-makers have followed an ideal: to make good wine that shows the terroir of the landscape and to make something individual, some remain content to play to global fashion. Simply put, thirty years ago in Britain and elsewhere medium-sweet white wine with low alcohol was popular and Germany cashed in big time on this fashion. Liebfraumilch became so ingrained in most peoples' minds as what came from Germany they overlooked the fine wines of the Mosel and Rhine and when Liebfraumilch went out of fashion and chardonnay became the new "must have" the German wine industry caught a cold. Once chardonnay was in fashion, all over the world vineyards owners who grew riesling or maybe some other less well known grape variety quickly dug up their vines and replanted their vineyards with chardonnay.

At first it was just plain chardonnay everyone wanted. Then they wanted "oaked" chardonnay. New World wine-makers quickly labelled subsequent vintages with the name of their vineyard and underneath the words "Oaked Chardonnay". A few years later the newspapers and magazines in their wine reviews told everyone that oaked chardonnay was no longer liked and people were demanding un-oaked chardonnay. Hey presto! The next vintages to be shipped from Australia and elsewhere carried labels with the key words "Un-oaked Chardonnay" written on them. By now the chaps who had ripped up their riesling and planted chardonnay had vines which were five years old and at last able to produce fruit that could be made into wine, so more immature and dull chardonnay poured into the market place.

I should mention at this point that, generally speaking, as vines get older, whilst they produce fewer grapes, the quality of the wine, its richness of flavour, is invariably better.

I remember one tasting where a good friend of mine, Adam Bancroft gave me the new vintage of a good producer of chardonnay from Australia to try. The vintage we had been stocking was labelled "un-oaked" whilst a couple of years before they had been making an oaked wine and labelling it such. I sniffed and tasted the new wine and looked at the label. To me the wine tasted as if it had been very lightly oaked, but no indication of whether it was oaked or not, was given on the label.

'So he's not saying on the label whether it is oaked or not?' I commented.

'He's not sure which way things will go next year so he's hedging his bets by saying nothing,' Adam answered.

Adam later sold me pinot noir from a top notch Australian winery: truly first rate. I bought the pinot and clients loved it, then suddenly it ceased to be available. Adam's answer was succinct but like me I could sense his disappointment.

'Australian pinots haven't been having good press lately and there's more demand for cabernet so they've ripped up the vineyard and replanted it.'

This merry-go-round by vineyard owners chasing after the fashionable grape varieties has gone on for too long now and too many beautiful old vines, including many rare local grape varieties have been lost. Thankfully at last, unusual, regional grape varieties are becoming far more appreciated. Vineyard growers are also waking up to the fact that if their vineyard is ideal for growing pinot gris rather than sauvignon blanc then pinot gris is what they should grow and they need to be proud of it.

Just as with white grape varieties certain red wine grape varieties have enjoyed fashion favour. But keep in mind the grape variety is just one point from which the creation of wine comes: location, vinification methods and, most crucially perhaps, the attitude and skill of the wine-maker, all play their part in how the wine ends up tasting. This is so easily proved when you taste two wines made from the same grape variety grown side by side and one tastes like chalk and the other tastes like cheese.

Adam Bancroft, from whom I had the pleasure of buying wines, was a modest, unassuming chap; when tasting something would seldom say more than, "very good, will be better in a couple of years", or would offer a wine for me to buy with, "I bought a load of this when I was in Piedmont but I now think having re-tasted it, it's too tough, but I thought you may be able to use it if I knock three quid a bottle off?'

Adam was a Master of Wine and discovered quite a few wines that went on to international acclaim. He basically only bought however from France, Italy, Australia and New Zealand. He only listed one modest property in Bordeaux and when I asked why he didn't list more he looked faintly sheepish and shrugged and just said; "They don't really interest me." Through him I discovered grape varieties and regions I had previously had no awareness of; I greatly respected his palate which was very perceptive. He seldom used adjectives like blackcurrants or gooseberries and tasting great wines with him I noticed that he would sometimes do nothing more than sip, spit and nod with satisfaction. Sadly Adam died far too young. Just for reference there is another wine company on the go called Bancroft but the common name is the only connection.

In the 1960's and 70's and even 1980s because of the vagaries of weather the regions of Bordeaux and Burgundy tended to make really good wine about one vintage in every three. It was in those days imperative to learn about the vintages. The wines were also made to mature quite slowly and if they did not taste appealing when young this was not considered a problem, it was assumed you would be drinking wine from an older vintage.

Back in these days when visiting the French vineyards just before or just after the harvest if you asked the vignerons for their views about the quality of the vintage the responses were invariably easy to translate:

"This could turn out to be one of our best vintages" generally meant: "A good vintage"

"Early indications make us confident that this vintage will make lovely wines, approachable in their youth and displaying great charm" invariably really meant; "A dull vintage, best drunk young and forgotten about."

"Despite the problems we have had with this year I think we have done really well" was the usual answer which generally covered up the vigneron's real thoughts which were; "We will do really well if we can manage to hood-wink some dumb foreigner like you into actually paying us for this."

In Rioja, across in Spain, such manipulation of the truth was regarded as utterly unacceptable. If a vintage was a bad vintage it was declared bad. If it was great it was lauded as such. Curiously, however, even if one searched hard for a bottle from a bad vintage they were impossible to find but at least miraculously there seemed to be plenty of availability from the great vintages. How very fortuitous.

Bordeaux

I started my exploration of fine red wine back in the late 1970s with Bordeaux. It was my first love. Since then I have become frustrated by the region. My tastes in wine have doubtless changed but so too has the style in which Bordeaux is made. I'll explain this in more detail in a moment but first let's deal with the obvious questions: what does Bordeaux taste like? Why is it so famous?

Bordeaux is a medium weight red wine with a dry after taste. The fruit is typically described as blackcurrant and it should have a rich bouquet which nicely balances fruit smells along with other smells. My tasting notes frequently referred to cedar, cigar boxes, oak and such like. I think the wine goes well with roast lamb. I like the wine with some age and I'd expect to drink a bottle of Bordeaux when it's ten or twenty years old.

The heart of the Bordeaux region was an inhospitable marsh until Dutch engineers set to work draining it in the 17th century. Centuries earlier the most famous wine region of south west France was Cahors, not Bordeaux. Bordeaux grew as a port and centre of commerce with the French colonies; it had been a centre for wine making in the late medieval days with pockets of vineyards around the walled city, it's red wines then were so pale and feeble as to be described as clairet (rosé practically), hence claret as a term was applied. In 1453 the English lost control of Bordeaux to the French and exports of claret to England fell to around a tenth of what they had been a hundred years before.

After the Dutch engineers had drained the marshes in the heart of the Bordeaux region the land started to be turned over to the cultivation of vines. The gravel soil proved ideal and the climate was pretty much spot on for gently ripening grapes over the growing season. Wealthy investors moved in and by the middle of the nineteenth century the vineyards of Bordeaux, or more specifically, the Medoc region in the centre of the Bordeaux area had established a reputation for making very good wines.

In 1855 all the properties making wine were evaluated based on the prices they'd been fetching and a league table was formalized with a few properties ranked 1st[t] Growths at the pinnacle and then below them there were some 2nd Growths and below these 3rd Growths and so on. The original Bordeaux classification system of 1855 remains pretty much as it was back then. There were four 1st Growths originally but a Chateau called Mouton Rothschild got promoted from 2nd to 1st Growth and that has been about the only change to affect this league table in over a hundred and fifty years. All the top wine making properties now sell their wines for a lot of money; the top wines vie for the attention of the super-rich and because these people can pay whatever it takes to buy a bottle, prices are pushed relentlessly upwards. Such is the value of these wines now that cases of top Bordeaux are traded as investment commodities by financial speculators in much the same way as fine art.

Back in the 1980s a good bottle of Bordeaux only cost about four times the price of a cheap bottle of plonk. Nowadays a bottle of good Bordeaux will cost ten or twenty times the price of a bottle of plonk. A top notch

Bordeaux will set you back even more and for the price of one bottle you could easily buy a hundred bottles of decent wine from elsewhere. Inflation has gone at one speed whilst the price of the finest Bordeaux has shot up at a meteoric rate in comparison.

The style of Bordeaux has changed over the last thirty years as well. Nowadays top wines are subject to such international scrutiny and evaluation that the great Chateaux will spare no expense or effort to make wine better than their neighbours. What the typical international consumer of today wants from his bottle is not what was wanted three or four decades ago. To over simplify things: a hundred years ago most Bordeaux was drunk by the French or exported to Britain, Germany, the Low Countries and Scandinavia. Now the majority of top end Bordeaux is bought by citizens of the United States of America, China and Russia. Not to labour a point, but, at the outset of the First World War a hundred years ago most bottles of Bordeaux were being served with roast beef and roast lamb in the grand houses of the well-heeled and would be probably preceded by some fish, washed down with a glass of white Burgundy and the meal would most likely be rounded off with some cheese and a glass of port. Fast forward to today and for some curious reason most Bordeaux is made more in a style that is closer to Californian cabernet sauvignon. Fashions change: in the 1960's sports cars looked sleek and elegant whereas today 4x4s are fashionable and they look, to my mind, more like armoured vehicles than sports cars. Nothing wrong with that and given the state of driving on today's roads, an armoured car makes sense.

The most influential wine critics today are American because they have the biggest target audience and since their audience appreciates, shall we say, different characteristics in their wines, the Bordeaux estates have subtly over the last few decades adjusted the style in which they make their wines to meet the style expectations of their audience. I have a sneaking feeling that if Russia and China continue to expand as markets for fine Bordeaux then there will be another subtle shift in style to pander to their particular tastes. When Louis Roederer Crystal was first made for the Russian Imperial Court is was sweet because that is what they demanded. When the Czar was executed and Roederer lost its best client it switched its focus of attention to elsewhere. Britain wanted Champagne but bone dry Champagne, so Crystal went from sweet to dry. The Czar had been happy to pay for his Champagne in crystal bottles hence the name but the British were not so fussed about packaging so Crystal was henceforth bottled in plain glass but retained the name Crystal.

In Bordeaux 1982 was hailed as a great vintage and it was perhaps a pivotal year for the region. From 1855 until 1914 Bordeaux did well. However the First World War, then the Wall Street crash and prohibition in the United States and after that the Second World War all took their toll. After the Second World War few people had money to invest in making fine wine and priorities lay elsewhere. The Bordeaux Chateaux saw little investment during the fifties and sixties. In the sixties for every good vintage there seemed to be two bad vintages. The stock market crash and oil crisis in the early 1970s again affected Bordeaux heavily and the prices that Bordeaux could command slumped. If there was ever a bargain to be had in Bordeaux, it was buying the great 1970 vintage and good 1971 vintage a few years after they were made and the prices were ludicrously modest. At that time even the great vintages of the previous decade could be bought for very little.

As wine making embraced modern technology and

wine making became more scientific the quality of wines gradually became more consistent year on year. Global warming perhaps has also given a helping hand. Whilst fifty years ago vintages from a region such as Bordeaux could be variously ranked as: excellent, very good, good, average, below average and disappointing, the ranking now runs something like this: exceptional, excellent, very good, good, ideal for early consumption. In 1982 the top Chateaux of Bordeaux produced wines from a vintage that was truly excellent. By this time there were enough millionaires in the World interested in Bordeaux that the vintage was quickly sold out and suddenly people were eagerly awaiting the next great vintage. Chateaux began to invest more heavily in the use of new technology; there was a focus at the top end of striving for quality and perhaps also starting to take note of what buyers in the USA looked for when they bought a bottle of wine. During the eighties and nineties I believe the style of Bordeaux shifted subtly towards a more powerful and less subtle style of wine that echoed the style of red wine made from cabernet sauvignon vines grown in California. It was at this time that I started to explore cabernet sauvignon wines from elsewhere. I tried wines from California and Australia and the best were good for sure, but they didn't taste like Bordeaux.

One of the most exciting competitors to Bordeaux that I came across in the 1980s was a wine from a country that I had not even considered when thinking about places where wine might be made: the Lebanon.

Chateau Musar had not long arrived in the U.K. In 1979 the wine was tasted at the Bristol Wine Fair by Michael Broadbent and Roger Voss, two notable wine critics. They singled out the Chateau Musar 1967 as the most exciting wine out of everything on offer that year at the fair.

The vineyards of Musar had been first planted in the Bekaa valley in 1930 by Gaston Hochar, his son Serge had gone to Bordeaux University to study viticulture. The vineyard was planted with cabernet sauvignon and grape varieties associated with the Rhone valley and the Mediterranean coastal areas.

At the time I became a convert to this remarkable wine, Musar was being distributed by Rosemount the Australian wine producers and it was shipped along with their wines and warehoused at a bonded warehouse near Bristol. A bonded warehouse is a place where wines can be stored upon import to the U.K. but the importer can avoid paying the duty until the wine is then subsequently moved out of the warehouse. The advantage to the shipper, given that duty is about ten quid a case, is that if you ship a pallet of wine (about 50 cases) or a container of wine (more like 50 pallets) you can save having to pay out a small fortune in tax before you have even started to sell the wine. Much fine wine is actually bought in-bond which means one person buys it from another without it ever leaving the bonded warehouse and without the duty being paid.

Anyway at this time I was shipping wines which I'd found and liked and using the same bonded warehouse. I had been congratulating myself on shipping the likes of Chinon, Saumur Champigny and Gaillac which then seemed pretty much off the beaten track. The idea of a wine from Lebanon was to my mind outrageously romantic and after tasting the vintages that were being sold on the high street, the 1978 and the 1981 if I remember correctly, I called Rosemount and asked if I could buy five cases duty paid and would collect them myself from the bond as I needed to get some Gaillac out of the bond for a client who was so taken with it he'd just ordered ten more cases. With the back seat of my hatchback dropped down I could get twenty four cases in the car if I put one in the front foot well and one on the front passenger seat. Rosemount said no problem, then almost as a throw-away comment, the lady on the phone said:

"I don't suppose you'd be interested in some older wines would you?'

'Maybe,' I answered, suddenly feeling as if I might have stumbled across a treasure map or the key to a long lost vault.

'Well, it's just that we shipped a few cases of older vintages a while back and there are a few cases left.'

'What vintages are they?' I asked as if I had an intimate knowledge of the quality of historic Lebanese vintages whilst in truth I couldn't have even pointed accurately to the Lebanon on a world map.

'Well, quite old actually…'

I should mention at this point back in those days bonded warehouses refused point blank to break open cases and handle odd bottles which meant transactions were by the whole case.

'Okay,' I replied patiently, 'what vintages are they?'

'1969 in bottles and 1967 in magnums.'

'How much?' I asked, unable to believe that there was still some of the 1967 wine which had so impressed Michael Broadbent.

She told me. It seemed cheap but then if the wines were now dull or had tired with age I was wasting my money.

'Okay, I'll take a case of both.'

With hindsight it is easy to realise that the Lebanon can make fine wine. The Bekaa valley provides high altitude slopes where there is over the year a perfect temperature for growing grapes, the Phoenicians knew this when they established vineyards there thousands of years ago.

When I arrived at the bonded warehouse I felt a child's

sense of anticipation when presented with wrapped Christmas presents as I loaded the cases into the back of my car. There were half a dozen loading bays with an articulated lorry backed up to each; a forklift truck was zipping around with a pallet of cases at a time.

The last time I had taken delivery of a pallet one of the fifty cases had been damaged. It was a case on the corner and now watching the break neck speed at which the forklift driver was working I could imagine what had probably happened. The fifty cases had come from the south of France: some Cotes du Roussillon, Minervois and Fitou. Of the fifty cases, the one I was most looking forward to receiving, was a case of magnums of old vines Fitou and of course this was the case that had got smashed. All six magnums meeting an abrupt and un-timely end thanks to a forklift kebab attack!

So now I carefully loaded the two cases of old Chateau Musar into the front of my car and then put in the back the five cases of the current vintage Musar, the ten cases of Gaillac and the one case I'd also bought from Rosemount: a case of their Roxburgh Chardonnay for a chap who had an all Australian wine list in a little restaurant in Scotland. I'd never tasted the Roxburgh Chardonnay but he told me it was fabulous and being an Aussie and a wine enthusiast I reckoned he'd know what was what. Back then I knew precious little about Australian wine as they were still breaking into the British market. I had got as far as trying Wynns Coonawarra wines and the quality convinced me I needed to explore further.

The lorry drivers parked up at the bonded warehouse watched with mild curiosity as I hand loaded the eighteen cases into my car.

'Expensive wines are they?'

I sensed some genuine puzzlement and curiosity. I

suppose it wasn't every day a chap in an Italian sports car turned up to collect a few cases of wine from bonded warehouse.

'No, not really.'

I decided to open a magnum of the 1967 at a tasting for clients a couple of weeks later. I sent out a few dozen invitations and a dozen people turned up. The tasting was a complete mix of wines ranging from Gaillac to Vosne Romanée. The 1967 Musar was first rate; mature but not tired; a lovely nose of cedar and spice and a taste that was both earthy and fruity with a sort of dusty character which I liked. This was perhaps the slightly rustic, local terroir of the place, and I am not using the word rustic in a derogatory way. Just as a marble mantle-piece with an ornate mirror in a Louis XIV style can be impressive so can a simply hewn oak timber also be impressive over an open fireplace. Anyway, I was stunned by the Chateau Musar and so was everyone else. There were a fistful of top notch French wines for tasting but everyone seemed distracted by the Musar and we were all quite amazed to be tasting this beautiful wine that had come out of an essentially Arabic and notionally tee-total country that had recently been ravaged by war.

Chateau Musar at this time was far less expensive than wines from Bordeaux of a comparable quality. It joined the ranks of a few other wines I had tasted that made me realise that Bordeaux wasn't the only place from which you could find great cabernet sauvignon.

After everyone had left the wine tasting I surveyed the remains in all the bottles. Of course people had been generally sipping and spitting but interestingly whilst most of the bottles were perhaps now half empty the magnum of Musar was barely a quarter full. I poured myself a glass of the Musar that evening and sat with it in front of the log fire at home. It was dramatically different to the Torres Gran Coronas Black Label but just like the Torres wine it held my attention and I loved it. Whilst the Torres had stood out as I said like a Jensen Interceptor in a car park, now I felt I had pushed open the door of an old barn and discovered a Jaguar XK under a layer of dust.

In the 1980s a certain small hotel was brought to my attention as it had amazing wines. When I tried to find out what was meant by this, people were vague to say the least.

"Oh, we heard from friends who have a friend who loves fine wines that he dines there because of the wines."

Curious, I promptly booked a table and went along with my girlfriend. From outside, the place looked depressingly dull being sandwiched between two shops on the high street of a sleepy little town that was sadly down at heel. Inside, the lounge bar seemed very out of date and was all but deserted. An elderly but imposing man in a starched white waiter's jacket greeted us and took our drinks order. The menu was brought; typed on card embossed with the name of the hotel and with the day's date on it. I read the menu and my heart sank. It offered a rudimentary choice of three starters, three main courses and three desserts. It read like something out the 1950's and I was convinced we were in for a depressing evening. We opted for smoked salmon then roast beef as there was nothing more interesting or unusual. I had by this point decided that someone was having a laugh or we had got the wrong hotel.

I then asked to see the wine list. The elderly gentleman, who I later found out was the owner, sniffed and looked down at me and said with considerable gravitas;

"I do not have a wine list; what sort of wine would interest you?'

"Bordeaux," I answered.

"Yes," he answered, "I have Bordeaux from 1970:

Chateau Leoville Poyferre, Chateau de Pez and Chateau la Riviere."

He looked at me with that sort of deferent look that is bestowed by someone who actually makes you feel not only that they are doing you favour by looking after you, but in fact you are hardly worth their attention. He stood, as straight backed as a sergeant major and remained smugly silent.

I did some quick thinking about my budget as he had not made any reference to price. At this time the excellent 1970 vintage was still to be found in a few wine merchants lists but it came at a price. As hotels and restaurants generally tripled the price they bought at, to set their selling price, I realised I was in for a hefty night out. I knew Chateau La Riviere was from a little known commune called Fronsac and was probably the least impressive of the three wines. Chateau de Pez, a Cru Bourgeois St Estephe, I reckoned was in the middle of the three as far as price and quality were concerned. I was certain the Leoville was going to cost an arm and a leg so I plumped for the de Pez.

We were then shown upstairs to the dining room and we found that we were the only guests dining. The dining room had perhaps a dozen tables, each with a starched white cloth, gleaming silver cutlery, fresh flowers and a lit candle. A dear old waitress brought us bread, water and served our meal. The only sound was the gentle ticking of a mantelpiece clock. The owner served the wine which was decanted. It was, as I had anticipated, very good. The beef turned out to be roast fillet and the portions were very generous. We took coffees in a lounge upstairs, which was again deserted and had the feel and décor or a first class cocktail lounge on board a cruise ship from the 1930's.

When the bill came the Chateau de Pez was ludicrously cheap. It would have cost much more had I found a bottle in a wine shop. I promptly re-booked for a fortnight later. We drank the 1970 Chateau Leoville Poyferre and on the bill it too was priced ridiculously low and oddly at the very same amount as the de Pez. I told a friend who was a wine merchant what I had paid for it and he commented that one would probably pay more at auction if one could still get it and he certainly didn't now have any stocks of the 1970 vintage left.

We went back a third time. The owner welcomed us with a faint smile and I asked him what he thought of the Chateau La Riviere.

'For a lesser Chateau it is actually very good and it is drinking very well.'

'Then let's try it,' I answered.

He was right; the wine was good.

This time our cheerful waitress was kept busy as there was another table of two also dining; an elderly couple who were on a motoring holiday. The other gentleman dining asked for a wine list and was given the same answer. The guest hesitated then looked around for support. His wife was suddenly fascinated by the ceiling and all I could do was offer a smile from where I sat sipping my gin and tonic.

"Well, I do like Burgundy..." the man ventured.

"I have three," the reply came like a rifle shot. Silenced followed for a few seconds for dramatic effect. By now I was coming to the conclusion that the owner liked things in three's: starters, main courses, Clarets, Burgundies.

"I have a Fleurie from 1976, a Chambolle Musigny from 1974 and a Clos Vougeot from 1971."

Logically I reckoned that there was no way these wines would all be the same price. The Grand Cru Clos Vougeot should be around five or six times the price of the Fleurie which whilst it might well be enjoyable was at the end of the day a top notch Beaujolais Villages but nothing more and certainly wasn't going to compete with a Grand Cru from one of the great communes of the Cote d'Or.

The gentleman ordered the Beaujolais Villages. We drank our claret, ate our roast lamb and I felt pretty close to heaven. A few weeks later when we went back again we were welcomed practically like old friends and when I ordered the Chambolle Musigny the owner gave a knowing nod of approval. Once again the price was the same. The Chambolle Musigny was very seductive and a return to try the Clos Vougeot was already in my mind whilst I was savouring the last mouthful of Chambolle.

In recent years the most interesting and informative tasting of Bordeaux that I have been to was hosted by Christian Moueix the owner of Chateau Petrus. Petrus is perhaps the most expensive of all Bordeaux properties. There were ten guests invited and the tasting was half a dozen vintages from one of the other Pomerol properties owned by Moueix. These wines were eye wateringly expensive but still only a fraction of the price of Petrus. Monsieur Moueix was charm personified and very modest about his wines, modest but serious. Upon tasting the first wine he noted, quite calmly, that the temperature the wine had been presented at was higher than the ideal temperature at which he believed his wines should be served. The room, a Michelin starred restaurant in a five star hotel, was indeed warm, and in his mind too warm. I have to say that I agreed with him.

What I found most interesting that day was that the 2005, which was technically a perfect vintage and generally hailed as the best vintage since 1945, was less impressive than another supposedly less stunning vintage. Even allowing for the consideration of the age of the vintage and that it may still be developing, there was a strong feeling amongst the ten guests, all of whom were professionals in the wine business, that the wine was somewhat disappointing and that the bottle from another vintage was, in comparison, surprising by its superiority.

I suppose this goes to show that until you pull the cork and drink the wine you cannot be absolutely certain of what lies in store.

Whilst I do feel that Bordeaux generally no longer offers value for money it does undeniably offer a great choice of great wines. A few Chateaux that I have always enjoyed and have a soft spot for are:

Chateau Larcis Ducasse, Grand Cru St Emilion. I first tried this wine from the 1976 vintage and I thought it charming. It's had its ups and downs since then but since 2002 it has been owned by Nicolas Thienpont and the famous Stéphane Derenoncourt has been consultant. The vineyard has a high proportion of cabernet franc and a very low proportion of cabernet sauvignon. The main grape variety is merlot.

Chateau Roc des Cambes, Cotes de Bourg. This property is in a commune that is regarded as not up to very much but the wine is really good and proves that generalisations can be over-turned.

Chateau Smith Haut Lafitte, Grand Cru Graves. I've tried vintages on and off since the 1970s and have enjoyed them. There's a good white (which has a dash of sauvignon gris in its mostly sauvignon blanc plus a splash of Semillon blend) as well as good red which is fairly priced. The vineyard has gone organic too, and they have their own barrel maker which I like the idea of.

Chateau Gloria, Cru Bourgeois St Julien. In 1942 Henri Martin, the Mayor at the little town of St Julien bought a few acres of vines from a great Chateau that perhaps in such dire times was pleased to have the cash. Henri Martin went on to buy a few vines here and there from half a dozen other great estates. He finally bought some cellars and started wine making. His father had been a barrel maker at the famous Chateau Saint Pierre and in the Haut Medoc where everything had been set in stone in 1855, Martin had effectively created a new Chateau by acquiring parcels of vines here and there where the great Cru Classé estates were willing to sell. Martin called his wine Chateau Gloria although there was and is no Chateau. The label features angles with giant trumpets and I bet this is how he felt as his wine became famous. In 1982, aged seventy-eight Martin had done well enough to even buy the Chateau Saint Pierre where his father had worked as barrel maker.

Bordeaux also produces small quantities of dry white wine from mostly semillon and sauvignon blanc grape varieties. One or two of the top Chateaux for serious red wine make small quantities of very good dry white wine but it is very expensive.

Sauternes and Barsac are two communes further inland that when autumn conditions are right can make fabulous dessert wine from late harvested grapes that have undergone what is called noble rot. Simply put the autumn morning mists can create an ambient atmosphere that kick starts a specific type of mould which affects the grapes. This rot, unlike others, does not affect the taste but it does make the grapes shrivel and this concentrates the sugars. The wine that is then made is very sweet.

There are some other areas around the world which can produce sweet wines that have also been made in this way:

parts of Germany, Austria, other parts of France, one small region in Hungary called Tokai, parts of Austria, Canada even and doubtless somewhere else, which I have forgotten and for which I must apologise.

Sauternes and Barsac have had a reputation for making fabulous dessert wines for centuries and whilst the wines are expensive they are relatively speaking in my mind under-priced. The grapes do not all rot conveniently at the same time so instead of being able to harvest all the grapes in one go the vineyards have to be re-visited several times. Assessing the grapes before picking requires a trained eye, so these vineyards are always hand-harvested by seasoned pickers and the best properties will send the grape pickers into the vineyards sometimes half a dozen times. Costs for making the wine continue to escalate since the grapes are yielding smaller amounts of juice a proportionately smaller amount of wine is made. All of this to my mind should make sweet white Bordeaux far more expensive than red Bordeaux. However red Bordeaux is in high demand internationally and sweet white Bordeaux is not, so Sauternes and Barsac remain, relatively speaking, a bargain. The finest wine is without doubt made at Chateau d'Yquem and it is certainly not on offer at a give-away price but have a look at a map and pick the wine from one of d'Yquem's neighbours such as Suduiraut and for a fraction of the price you will have bought yourself a first rate bottle of truly fine sweet wine. Don't drink the wine too young though: the best vintages take a decade or two to develop. I bought a couple of bottles of Suduiraut 1962 and a couple of the 1967 vintage in the 1970s for under £4 a bottle. I drank the last bottle in 1984 and it was magnificent. I noticed in an auction catalogue some still for sale in the late 1990s with an estimated reserve price of £90 a bottle. I think since then, as the wines are now fully mature, the prices have come down a little.

One last consideration is that because the wine is so luscious it is a wine that begs to be sipped and enjoyed in just small quantities so a single bottle can be easily shared around at a dinner party for eight whereas a good bottle of red Burgundy, I find, is barely enough for a dinner for two.

Some interesting alternatives to Sauternes or Barsac with more modest price tags, if you move outside of the Bordeaux region, are Monbazillac, Coteaux de Layon (made from the chenin blanc grape variety), late harvest Vouvray (also made from the chenin blanc grape variety) and from the far south west of France Jurancon (made from the petit menseng). Jurancon also makes good, dry white wine. Sweet wines from Alsace are well worth exploring; riesling and gewurztraminer grape variety are used to make dessert wines and these wines are labelled Vendange Tardive or Selection des Grains Nobles. Bonnezeaux and Quarts de Chaume are fabulous. Both are made on the Loire from chenin blanc grapes. From outside France the choice widens: Germany and Austria make fabulous lusciously sweet wines, frequently from the riesling grape, but from other varieties as well.

German Trockenbeerenauslese labelled wines are super sweet; Beerenauslese means very sweet; Auslese will be sweet; Spatlese will be very fruity, almost sweet; Kabinett wines are generally medium dry and wines labelled Trocken are dry.

Other countries that spring to mind for luscious, dessert wines are Italy, Canada and recently I tasted a Portuguese late harvest white that was really good.

Sooner or later if you love sweet wine, you'll have to taste Tokai Aszu from Hungary. Love it or hate it the wine is stylistically individualistic and the sweetest examples are probably sweeter than anything else one can find.

Surrounding the main fine wine areas of Bordeaux are outlying vineyards and these are generally of more modest quality and the wines sell for a far more sensible price. On the opposite side of the Gironde to the Haut-Medoc are the vineyards of Bourg and Blaye. These are modestly priced wines but well situated properties which, if they have a mind to, can produce very good wines indeed.

The commune of Fronsac is also worth investigating and even within the Haut-Medoc there are good and more modestly priced wines to be found. Listrac and Moulis are two communes which have plenty of good Chateaux whose wines are not priced out of the reach of ordinary wine drinkers like you or me.

So to conclude: Bordeaux does offer great wine but at a price. There are however numerous regions and individuals around the world who are making wines in a not dissimilar style you may find great pleasure in more modestly priced wines from a host of growers from other countries or from elsewhere within France.

Burgundy

The Burgundy wine region is small and famous. Its fame rests on the fact that at its best the region makes wines that are truly great; these generally come from the heart of the region, from the Cote d'Or. The red wines of Burgundy are made from pinot noir grapes and the white wines are made from chardonnay grapes.

The Cote d'Or, the golden slope, is a line of low hills which forms a ridge and is the heart of Burgundy. To me, they look very ordinary, quite dull and hardly worth a second glance. This narrow, gentle ridge runs roughly south-west to north-east and the vineyards of note are all on the east facing side. The geology of the ridge is complex but the combination of soil types in the proportions that can be found here, combined with the climate, create an opportunity with the right grape varieties: pinot noir for red wine and chardonnay for white wine, as just mentioned, to make gorgeous wines. Style and complexity are the benchmarks of Burgundy when the grapes are grown, nurtured, harvested and made into wine with skill by wine makers who are passionate about their craft.

Of course there are more mediocre vineyards. There are even very good vineyards that are treated in a casual manner by their owners and there are still wine-makers who are complacent because they know they have a ready market for their wines. All of this can mean that there are still lack-lustre wines to be found.

Burgundy is lovely; I love Burgundy when it's well made but often bottles are disappointing and this is in no part due to the price tag. Burgundy is expensive and indeed pinot noir grown anywhere in the world is frequently expensive because it is a low cropping, fickle grape that needs very precise climatic conditions to reveal its true potential. Chardonnay, the white grape of Burgundy is grown widely outside of Burgundy. In fact it is grown just about everywhere. Chardonnay can be cheap or expensive depending on where it is grown. However chardonnay grown in Burgundy is never cheap. At best it is affordable and it worst when you start to look for bottles from Grand Cru vineyards it becomes eye-watering costly.

What does Burgundy taste like? Why is it considered so good? What should it taste like? Every wine enthusiast will have their own answer for this and there are plenty of informed answers to be found for these simple questions. For me, red Burgundy when it's good is soft, warm, tantalising, almost hinting at something sweet. It brims with fruit and tastes so velvety that I can practically guzzle it in large mouthfuls. However it also has layers of perfumed aroma which hints at spices and forests. Whilst some red wines command attention by their power or complexity, red Burgundy is seductive. White Burgundy at its best achieves a perfect balance between fruit flavours and minerality and it, or should be, a glass of wine that provokes thoughtful contemplation. It is a wine to sip with good food.

The entry level for basic red or white Burgundy is Bourgogne Rouge or Bourgogne Blanc. Next up comes wine made from grapes anywhere in the southern half or northern half of the Cote d'Or and this is called "Cotes de Beaune Villages" or "Cotes de Nuits Villages" respectively.

The next rank up is wine from grapes grown around specific villages; Santenay for example. The better vineyards will carry their own vineyard name which may be shown on the label and the best of these are usually ranked as "1er Cru". So instead of a more humble bottle of Santenay you might come across a bottle of "Santenay 1er Cru Les Gravieres". There is one rank higher than 1er Cru and that is Grand Cru. The Grand Cru vineyards may have their name hyphenated to the vineyards of a village commune so that the whole village may bask in some reflected glory. Only 5% of Burgundy is ranked as Grand Cru; there are thirty-two such vineyards. The wines are very expensive but are frequently superb, if you get to drink them at their peak. By at their peak I mean when they taste their best. White Burgundy can be a bit fickle and a few years after it is bottled it can often behave like a sulky teenager and offers little satisfaction. Red Burgundy depending on where the wine is made can take a few years to develop, or longer if from a good vineyard or it may take a decade or more if it is from Grand Cru vineyard. Drinking it when it is too young is usually as rewarding an experience as buying a mango from a supermarket. However leave Burgundy too long and you will be left with something about as appealing as a microwave supper that has been cooked for eight minutes instead of four. Timing is everything.

To the south of the Cote d'Or there are more vineyards in the regions of the Cotes Chalonnais and the Cotes Maconnais. Some people regard these regions as all part of Burgundy but others don't. The best of these wines are hugely enjoyable and they won't, by and large, break the bank. Pouilly Fuissé is one of the best known but is not to be confused with Pouilly Fumé. The former is made from chardonnay grapes to the south of Burgundy and the latter is made from sauvignon blanc grapes grown far to the north, on the Loire. The former perhaps offers the satisfaction of a Volvo saloon whilst the latter offer the fun of a Mazda soft-top. But remember, wines, like cars, are a question of personal taste.

When you buy a bottle of Burgundy there will be three key facts that you'll be looking for on the wine label. First is the name of the village and or the vineyard from where the grapes come. The second is the name of the person who has made the wine. The third is the vintage - the year in which the grapes were harvested. Because the climate here is very marginal for making fine wine, the quality of the vintage, the weather in that particular year, is pretty critical. The name of the person that goes on the label is mostly nowadays the same person who owns the vineyard where the grapes were grown. In such instances assuming the proprietor bottles his wine at his own property as well, the label will say "Mise en bouteille au domaine"

There are though some big firms (negociants) operating in Burgundy who buy grapes from different sources and them make wine from them. These big outfits are far more consistent and better than they used to be say, fifty years ago but some are still a bit dull. Fifty years ago most Burgundy was bottled by these negociants but now most Burgundy is domaine bottled. Burgundy estates pass from father to son or daughter but if there are several children quite often the estate gets chopped up. As each member of the family will have his or her own ideas on how to make wine, the style of a domaine might change from generation to generation. Keeping track of who owns what and what their style of wine is like is a right headache.

Whilst, as I mentioned, the negociant wines are seen a lot less these days, some are certainly worth searching out. A typical negociant whose wines I once disliked and now I admire is Bouchard Pere et Fils. After a gradual decline over many years and lack lustre performance the firm was revitalised in 1995. They own around three hundred acres of land and have contracts to buy grapes from scores of small growers. They have built a state of the art new winery and have cellars where over 4,000 barrels are stored. This is seriously large scale production for the region. I tasted a dozen or more of their wines in 2010 and they were all good.

Alex Gambal at Beaune is at the other end of the scale. Alex is an American and after hearing things about this new little outfit being run out of Beaune by a chap from New York, I was intrigued. When I visited in 2008 to taste his 2006 wines his quantities were a trifle smaller than the likes of Bouchard. A Bourgogne Chardonnay sourced from vines at Savigny and 20% aged in new oak tasted really good, but there were only twelve barrels. A Bourgogne Rouge from vines at Volnay was again very good given its modest classification. Of course both these were examples of a wine-maker choosing to down play his product: the white could have been labelled Savigny Les Beaune and red Volnay but instead they were both sold as wines of a lower classification. This is not an uncommon practice amongst serious wine-makers.

Most Burgundy domains are small, production is limited and frequently the best wines are set aside for loyal clients. The great vineyards are often divided up amongst many families and it is quite common for a wine-maker to have only just enough vines to make a few barrels of a particular wine. *Hudelot Noellat in Chambolle* is one example. Tasting a 2006 Richbourg Grand Cru at the cellars I complimented Alain Hudelot upon the wine and asked how much he had made.

'Four and half a barrels.'

'What's the price?' asked the English wine shipper I was with.

'A hundred and thirty four euros a bottle.'

'Could you put me down for three cases (thirty six bottles) please,' replied the wine shipper.

Alain shook his head negatively.

'I can spare you six bottles; it's all I have left.'

And this is a wine that will not be ready to drink for ten years. So the obvious question that comes next is; can you find good wines made from pinot noir from places other than Burgundy? The answer is yes.

California tried making fine wine from the pinot noir grape but the climate, at first, seemed too hot. Other countries tried and also failed. Burgundy for red wine seemed impregnable. Then someone in Oregon fancied their climate was more akin to Burgundy and they tried their luck. The wine was good; with each successive vintage, as the vines matured and the wine maker grew more familiar with the grapes he was dealing with, the wines of Oregon tasted better. Other wine-makers started looking for the golden chalice of a perfect climate and perfect soil for this most problematical of grape varieties. A chap called Andrew Pirrie started a vineyard in Tasmania which had a cool climate not dissimilar to that of Burgundy. The wine he made was good and wine makers all around the globe set off on the quest for a cool climate and location suitable for growing pinot noir. Pushing the boundries of "cool climate" seemingly as far as they would go, someone even set up shop in the far south of New Zealand in the Otago region.

Californian wine-makers now believed that Burgundy could be emulated, but the starting point had to be a cooler climate than where all their current vineyards were, thus the search for suitable sites began. The choices seemed to be developing vineyards closer to the coast where it was cooler or moving well inland and planting vineyards at a higher altitude where it would also be cooler. Joe Rochioli and Howard Allen successfully established good vineyards in the Russian River region. In the 1990s Californian wine makers were also seriously reflecting upon Burgundian wine-making practices and were beginning to realise that, if what seemed rustic worked and sometimes high-tec failed, then they needed to consider their options. Methods such as using open-top fermenters were experimented with. Au Bon Climat estate started to buy pinot fruit from vineyards in Santa Barbara and although the vines were young, the wines showed potential. The Anderson Valley became recognised as an ideal cool climate for pinot noir and this area received an amazing endorsement when Louis Roederer Champagne set up shop here to make a sparkling wine to compete with Champagne.

In general terms, much Californian pinot noir has evolved from something chunky, powerful and alcoholic to something more restrained, complex and with slightly lower alcohol levels. That said, most Californian pinot noir is still a more alcoholic and heavy weight brew than what the French achieve. I liken a lot of Californian wine-making to something similar to the Mustang philosophy of making a car fast: simply put a very large engine in and away you go. If Burgundy wine-makers have always needed to keep their fingers crossed and hope for enough sunshine throughout the growing season to achieve good ripeness, then in California the challenge has been to achieve subtlety and elegance, as there is invariably enough sunshine to produce grapes that will make wine laden with alcohol and with a tendency towards low acidity. Pinot noir at its most thrilling is almost a question of "less is more"; so rather than starting with a massive engine the art of wine-making is achieving performance without relying on brawn.

To over-exaggerate the issue of too much sunshine, keep in mind that some hot countries grow grapes but don't produce wine only raisins.

Some of the many Californian makers of good pinot noir that you might like to look out include: Flowers, Kistler, Joseph Phelps and Cobb in Sonoma; Breggo and Goldeneye in Mendocino and Au Bon Climat in Santa Barbara. Good pinot though comes at a price so for one bottle of decent pinot from California expect to pay the same, if not more, than what a decent bottle of Burgundy will cost.

Central Otago at the southern end of New Zealand's South Island was the region for pinot noir that first caught my attention however. In 2006 I tried a pinot noir from Otago that made me realise that whilst stylistically not at all like Burgundy, it was without doubt possible to make truly first rate pinot noir outside of Burgundy. The wine was Pisa Range.

Pisa Range vineyard was established by Warwick and Jenny Hawker in 1995 and the first vintage they bottled was the 2000. I think that they were the first people to plant vines in the Cromwell Basin sub-region. In terms of exploring the world of vineyards they'd just set up shop on the far side of the moon. They now have around ten acres of pinot as well as a small plot of riesling. The first vintage I tried was a 2003: a big, brooding wine, rich in fruit and with a gorgeous bouquet of spice and dark fruit, I was entranced. A decade on and a tasting by Decanter Magazine of Otago pinot's, ranks Pisa Range as the best that the region produces. I have since then enjoyed many pinot noir wines from different growers in Otago but Pisa Range remains my favourite.

Felton Road is perhaps the best known Central Otago pinot but I've not tasted it.

Pegasus Bay is like and tastes to my mind a bit like a full-blown old fashioned Vosne Romanée from a super-ripe vintage.

Further north in New Zealand is Martinborough. The region has really good growing conditions for pinot noir with a winning combination of ancient river terraces with free draining alluvial soil, a long, cool growing season and modest rainfall.

Ata Rangi is perhaps the most highly regarded and comes with an appropriate price tag.

Urlar is roughly half the price and tastes good to me.

Chile is now also producing some cooler climate pinot noirs and if you search out the single vineyard premium priced wines you should get a good wine at a reasonable price.

South Africa is also a country to watch.

Iona Estate is very good indeed and I've been following these wines since I first met Andrew Gunn, the owner, a few years back. The vineyards are planted on a plateau at an altitude of over 1,000 feet. You can see the Atlantic Ocean from the vineyard and it has the coolest of climates compared with rest of South Africa. It takes a couple of months longer for grapes to ripen up here than down in other Cape vineyards. The first vineyard plantings were only made in 1997 so the vines are young but as vintage follows vintage the wines keep moving up a notch. Vine age, greater understanding of his vineyard or pursuit of bio-dynamic viticulture may all play a part in this; I don't know.

I met up with Andrew again recently. Alongside his sauvignon blanc and pinot noir he is now making a really good red from a blend of other grape varieties of which he has very small parcels; this is called "One Man Band". He also makes a really classy chardonnay, tremendously elegant. His pinot noir tastes better than ever. I asked him for his thoughts on his wines and his response follows in the chapter: "Freshness and Purity".

So with all this global competition to Burgundy what has happened back in the France? What has happened in Burgundy itself? Burgundy fifty years ago was dominated by negociants; big, long established business who would buy the grapes from the grape growers and blend them together in their house style before bottling and then selling the wine with their negociants named emblazoned upon the bottle. The negociants had always enjoyed an easy market for their wines and they were, I feel, complacent because of a lack of any real competition. Growers realised that if they not only grew the grapes but they made the wine and sold it themselves they could earn themselves more money and have the satisfaction of turning their own grapes into their own wine.

A few decades ago there was a flourish of domaine bottled Burgundy. These wines were made by people who had always known how to grow grapes but who were just in the infancy of learning how to make wine. It was at this time that pinot noir competition from overseas arrived and Burgundy was caught on the back foot.

The Burgundian fight back has been a bit like a fight between Napoleon and all his enemies. For a while every wine writer for every newspaper seemed to be happy to herald a New World pinot noir that was better, in their view, than Burgundy. Such sweeping generalisations are of course nonsense. Nevertheless, exciting pinot noirs were coming onto the market from all over the place. In Burgundy, I imagine, there was certainly a feeling of extreme disquiet.

I wouldn't like to say when the Burgundian fight back started and who really led the way. A romantic, altogether made up version of what happened might be thus: half a dozen young Burgundian wine-makers are sat together having a long lunch and talking about what they all share in common: all their families are vignerons, wine-makers in Burgundy. They grumble about how the shining reputation of Burgundy has become tarnished and how all these foreign upstarts are embarrassing them by making wine that they have to reluctantly admit is acceptably good. They crack open more bottles with which to commiserate.

'You know, this wine is not so bad?' says one, regarding the bottle.

'It was the last vintage my grandfather made,' answers another, continuing, 'and he decided that year he would let nature take its course and he did as little as possible. He reckons it was the best wine he ever made.'

'And taste this one here: this wine is fantastic.'

'Ah, that was the first vintage I made,' concedes Marie, another of the six gathered around the table. 'I was so worried my father would ridicule my efforts, I checked over every single bunch of grapes that we picked and only used the ones that looked perfectly ripe.

'What about this? My God, this is a wine to be reckoned with!' exclaims another of the lunching party.

'Oh that; that was from the year when I thought I had pruned too much and we made half the amount of wine we usually make,' concedes a young man sat opposite.

'But Pierre, this wine is twice as good as you usually make!'

'You think... yes, I suppose, it is a good one.'

The six young vignerons all look at each other and nod thoughtfully. Then almost as one they stand up and announce that they need to get back to their vineyard as they have some serious work to do.

The renaissance in Burgundy has been astonishing. There has not been some misguided shift to trying to make pinot noir in a style to emulate the pinot noirs of elsewhere. There has not been an attempt to make wines in some new internationally requested style as might have happened. Quite simply what has happened is that some wine-makers up and down the Cote d'Or have quietly decided that they can do better and each year they have steadily raised their game. Others, similarly inspired, have followed suit.

Whilst Burgundy makes small quantities of wine compared with Bordeaux, for one reason or another, it has not been favoured by wine investors to the same extent and this has helped to keep the prices more sensible. However even as I write the international wine investors are becoming more interested in Burgundy and already the prices of the top estates are moving up. So if you fancy trying some Burgundy where do you start? Well wines from the Cotes de Beaune or Cotes de Nuits will be labelled as such and these are just about your most basic level of Burgundy. If you want to move up a notch look for a wine labelled with the name of a specific village. The most famous villages are listed below and I have indicated whether they are generally better for red or for white wine.

1. Meursault (white)
2. Chassagne Montrachet (white)
3. Puligny Montrachet (white)
4. Volnay (red)
5. Pommard (red)

6 Beaune (red)
7 Aloxe Corton (red)
8 Nuits St Georges (red)
9 Vosne Romanée (red)
10 Vougeot (red)
11 Chambolle Musigny (red)
12 Morey St Denis (red)
13 Gevrey Chambertin (red)

Wines from specific vineyards that are really good will be ranked 1er Cru with the name of the vineyard as well as the village on the label and if you are willing to pay a bit more you should try one of these. For example:

1 Puligny Montrachet 1er Cru Combettes

Wines that are truly stunning (or are supposed to be!) are ranked Grand Cru and they are so self-confident that all they put on the label is the vineyard name (and the winemakers name). For example:

2 Le Montrachet

Grand Cru wines are expensive. If you buy a bottle then check out the vintage and get advice on how long to keep it before you drink it.

There are two regions called Hautes Cotes de Beaune and Hautes Cotes de Nuits. These vineyard areas are "higher" geographically but not in terms of quality. They are situated on the reverse side of the escarpment of hills where Burgundy is made and they make wines that should always have a more modest price tag. I've not yet found a wine from here that I can enthuse about.

In amongst the famous villages there are however a few villages that make respectable wines but with more modest price tags. I would suggest that you explore these wines as you can find really good wine at a reasonable price. Some villages worth checking out are:

3 Santenay
4 Auxey Duresses
5 Monthélie
6 Ladoix Serrigny
7 Fixin

If you ever fancy a holiday tasting wine in one of Frances great wine regions, I'd choose Burgundy. I have always found Burgundians friendly and affable and most of the best winemakers are remarkably modest. The towns are small, pretty and easy to explore on foot, the villages are sleepy and the pace is slow. The main town of the Cotes de Beaune is called Beaune and the main town of the Cotes de Nuits is Nuits St Georges. It is a modestly sized place. The vineyards continue as far north as a village called Marsannay and a short drive after that and you are at Dijon. It is that simple. Beaune is small, charming and full of tourists in the late summer but if you visit at other times of the year it is so quiet and unassuming that it is hard to believe that the most expensive land in the world might be just over the old stone wall behind you and the vines there are the most valuable in the world.

The vineyards of Burgundy were being cultivated in medieval days. They were already famous and long established when Cardinal Richelieu was managing France for Louis XIII decades before the first Dutch settlers arrived in South Africa and two hundred years before vineyards were established in Australia or California. Noted below are a few wines that come to mind as noteworthy.

Domaine de la Romanée-Conti make stunning wines from their Grand Cru holdings with staggering price tags. I have drunk a La Tache from a great vintage and it is memorable but I didn't have to buy it so the wine slipped down all the more easily.

Arnoux Chopin, Comblanchen. A young, affable and enthusiastic grower who makes a good Nuits St Georges Blanc "Les Monts de Boncourt", some good Cotes de Nuits Villages from old vines and a rich, dark Nuits St Georges "Bas de Combe".

Domaine Pierre Morey, Meursault is one of Burgundy's pioneers of biodynamic practice. He has also been wine-maker for Domaine Leflaive for a great many years. His Batard Montrachet is first rate and even his simple Bourgogne Blanc is far from simple.

Jean Marc Millot, Nuits St Georges. Easy drinking, soft and juicy wines with a luscious Vosne Romanée "1er Cru Les Suchots".

Domaine de Comtes Lafon, Meursault. This to my mind is a show case domaine. They have vines in a dozen or more great vineyards spread between Meursault, Monthélie, Volnay and Chassagne-Montrachet including some vines planted in 1953 in Le Montrachet. René Lafon ran the estate until 1984 when he handed over to his son Dominique. There's six people employed in the vineyard and two in the cellar along with a couple in the office. The estate has been bio-dynamic since the mid-1990s. The first wine I tasted from this domaine was a Volnay "1er Cru Champans" 1982 and at that time the Champans wine was made from vines planted in 1922. "Classy" was the first adjective I wrote on my tasting notes.

Aymeric Mazilly makes a St Aubin "1er Cru Les Castets" which stood out from the crowd for me with a mineral and smoky bacon nose and a long, ripe finish.

Dominique Mugneret makes intense, rich and full blown Vosne Romanée "1er Cru Les Charmes" and a Nuits St Georges "1er Cru Les Boudots" that is big, soft and blowsy; nicely balancing sweet fruit and firm tannins. At the risk of going into purple prose: if Hudelot Noellat has the firmness and structure of a tulip then Dominique Mugneret wines are old English roses of the deepest red.

Further south still and you come to Beaujolais. This is a lovely region to meander through in your car; big, rolling hills and pretty villages and it's warmer than Burgundy. Here I feel the south of France almost begins. Before I talk about Beaujolais however, the last word on pinot noir, the great red grape of Burgundy can go to the owners of Pisa Range in New Zealand, whose wine first lured me from my unswerving loyalty to Burgundy.

A Journey into the Unknown
by Jenny and Warwick Hawker

"Established in 1995 Pisa Range Estate is a small family owned boutique vineyard. Located in one of New Zealand's most spectacular landscapes the Pisa district of the Cromwell Basin just 45mins from Queenstown. In 1995 there were no vineyard plantings in the district – in fact Central Otago winemaking at that time was described as 'winemaking on the edge'. With its continental climate, latitude of 45 degrees south, growing grapes to make fine wine was viewed as being marginal – particularly with the ever present threat of frosts.

Our local winemaking history really only goes back to the mid -1980s, very young compared to the century old traditions of our European counterparts making us one of the 'youngest' wine growing regions on the planet. We often get asked why we chose to plant pinot noir - the heartbreaker grape – and why did we venture into the 'unknown' (as New Zealand diplomats we had no knowledge of the vigneron's life). However, the early winemaking pioneers of Gibbston, Alexandra and Wanaka had discovered through trial and error that pinot noir did like this place. Our hearts ruled our heads – falling in love with our land setting us on this journey of discovery.

The New Zealand psyche is, that when told 'it won't work' our answer is likely to be 'we will find a way to make it work'. Through observation and application, together with the special people we work with, we've come to understand our little slice of paradise. After thirteen vintages we feel we are on the way to learning the art of making a decent wine, but it's going to be the next generation that will make truly outstanding pinot noir wines. With the combination of vine age, collective experience and professionalism that now exists in our industry the future looks very exciting.

Our love of fine wine, fine food and good company set us on this journey – the romance is still there.

Jenny & Warwick Hawker
December 2013

Beaujolais

Beaujolais thirty years ago was famous for its Beaujolais Nouveau; brought to prominence in Britain by a couple of chaps racing each other back to England with bottles of the new vintage only just bottled and ludicrously young. However the cheap and cheerful image of Beaujolais Nouveau has not really helped the region because in the north there are a handful of villages where really good wine is made and at a very affordable price.

Search out the best growers from villages such as St Amour, Brouilly and Moulin a Vent and you should find a very satisfying bottle of red wine: richly flavoured but with very supple tannins; a distinctive aroma of semi-dried dark fruit, a whiff of ripe cheese and something mineral – like wet slate. Just now I am drinking a Brouilly from old vines by Domaine Joubert and for the money it's a more satisfying bottle than most Burgundy from the Cote d'Or at the same money.

The rolling granite hills of the Beaujolais region don't use pinot noir to make red wine. They use a grape variety called gamay and globally there really isn't much gamay on the go. There is a bit in the Loire valley, there's a bit in the south of France and a bit outside France, but generally speaking gamay is a grape which no-one really believes in except some dedicated growers in Beaujolais.

The first time I went to Beaujolais during the wine harvest it was gorgeous weather and the rolling hills, vineyards and sleepy little villages looked enchanting. I was looking for the house of a particular grower whose wine I had been buying. I had driven up a winding lane, vines laden with bunches of plump, gamay grapes on either side of the lane. People picking grapes paused to watch me as I stopped the car and looked at my map. I could now see that the lane ended in a small house. The grower whose wines I'd tasted had a picture of a far grander property on his wine label, so I assumed that the house at the end of the lane was not his and I was lost. One of the grape pickers put down her basket and ran across to my car, waving frantically. Whilst all the other women in the group were dark haired, deeply tanned and looked French, the one now running towards my car was blonde and pale skinned. She pointed at my registration plate and was grinning from ear to ear.

'You're English! God, I'm so home-sick, none of them speak proper English. Please say something,' she demanded in a well-educated home-counties accent.

'What do you want me to say?' I asked, trying not to laugh.

'Oh, just say anything, I've been here for nearly two weeks and none of them speak English and I'm going mad. Do you listen to The Archers?'

'I've been driving around France for nearly a month... sorry. I haven't been able to get Radio Four since Chablis.'

'My back's killing me; I thought this would be fun,' she gave me an apologetic smile and wiped her bare forearm across her face. Her freckled skin was red from sun burn on her bare shoulders. 'Are you lost?'

I told her the name of the wine grower that I was looking for and she pointed at the house at the lane's end.

'That's the family I'm staying with.'

That evening I dined with the wine-maker and his family. A stew of hare with root vegetables was accompanied by juicy, almost sweet wine from Andre's own vineyard. When I mentioned that Andre's home didn't look much like the house pictured on his wine label he nodded in agreement and told me that was their old family home but they'd sold it back in the seventies during the recession and had bought a smaller property that was close by. Changing the picture on the label of their wine... he shrugged ambivalently and refilled our glasses; there were wines with made up names and fictitious drawings of properties so it didn't matter did it?

Champagne

Think of sparkling wine and you think of Champagne. Whilst other countries make sparkling wine, none have yet managed to create such an iconic product as Champagne. It is internationally regarded as the luxury drink for celebration.

The Champagne region can be simply divided into three geographical areas and there also happen to be three grape varieties used to make Champagne: chardonnay, pinot noir and pinot meunier. When looking for a bottle of Champagne to buy there is a ready selection of famous names to be found on the high street but keep in mind this: firstly, Champagne does not benefit from being stored in bright light conditions. Secondly the lavish advertising campaigns employed by the high profile names, often using celebrities to endorse their product, comes at a price and this has to be paid for, you will be paying towards this when you buy a bottle of such Champagne.

Obviously the proportions in which the three grape varieties are used in any particular Champagne will affect the flavour. A good starting point for finding the style of Champagne that you prefer could be to consider whether you have an inclination towards a Champagne where chardonnay is the predominant grape variety or whether you find the character of a more pinot noir driven

Champagne more to your taste. Champagne that is made exclusively from chardonnay grapes should be labelled Blanc de Blancs and if it is made exclusively from black grapes then it should be labelled Blanc de Noirs. Even though the grapes are black skinned the juice that is run off to be fermented is white. Most Champagne though is made from a blend of all three grape varieties. Most Champagne is also a blend of the wine of numerous years assembled to create a consistent house style rather in the same way that a malt whisky is usually assembled from a whole array of differing casks made and matured by the same distillery. If a vintage is put on a label expect it to be good but also keep in mind vintage Champagne can often need ten years or longer to show its potential.

The whole Champagne region is big: closing in 100,000 acres but the best vineyards are to be found around the cities of Reims and Epernay. In very general terms the area around Reims favours pinot and the vineyards around Epernay are predominantly chardonnay.

All the vineyards in the region receive a percentage rating and this dictates the price that the grapes from each vineyard are worth. The vineyards that receive a 100% rating are termed Grand Cru.

The well-known names such as Lanson, Bollinger, Veuve Clicquot and Moet et Chandon buy grapes from a host of growers and they make considerable quantities of wine. Moet make millions bottles of Champagne every year. Incidentally Moet being a Dutch name should be pronounced with a hard "t". Their super luxury cuvée, Dom Perignon was first launched in 1921. (Cuvée is a selection of grapes to create or reflect a certain style) Veuve Clicquot happens to be connected to Moet by dint of the fact that they are both part of the company called Louis Vuitton Moet Hennessy. Veuve Clicquot has a turnover in excess of a billion euros, just like Moet, and the success of these names as international brands is formidable.

Champagne has continued to be a very successful product and as it is dominated by a handful of massive firms who buy tons of grapes from the hundreds of growers who have tiny parcels of wine; Champagne has changed very little. That said two things have emerged. The first is that on the back of the success of Dom Perignon made by Moet et Chandon, all of the big Champagne houses now make a luxury cuvee for those who want it. Examples are Cristal from Roederer, Cuvée Sir Winston Churchill from Pol Roger and René Lalou from Mumm. What makes it different? Well, it always comes in a flashy bottle and it is always very expensive. Does it taste better? Yes. One of the best ever Champagnes that I have drunk was a magnum of Cuvée Sir Winston Churchill 1975. Does it taste better enough to justify its hefty price tag? Well, buy some and judge for yourself.

There have also recently been a few more small growers making their own Champagne, now perhaps following the lead set by the growers in Burgundy. Some of these can be found in the U.K. and they are worth investigating. Champagne again is essentially a branded product although the likes of Moet are real properties and they have a long and illustrious history they are nevertheless blenders; their grape juice coming from lots of different small-holders from whom they buy their grapes each year. However if you fancy trying Champagne made by a single grower who has done everything himself including growing the grapes then it's perfectly possible to find such wines with a little patience. When you buy a bottle you will at least have the satisfaction of knowing that you are paying just for the effort that has gone into making the Champagne rather than paying towards a massive marketing budget as well.

Champagne has been a formidably successful wine and the Champagne houses, unable to expand beyond the geographical boundaries of the Champagne region, have expanded their business by setting up wineries in other countries and making sparkling wine out in those places: USA and Australia to name but two. They have also taken to buying farmland in southern England where the same chalky sub soil as there is in Champagne re-emerges. Global warming is making southern England a far more viable wine region now. Some English people have realised what is now possible and there are a handful of wine estates in England that instead of growing German style hybrid varieties that people planted thirty years ago have now been planted with the same grape varieties that are used in Champagne: chardonnay and pinot noir as well as a third called pinot meunier.

Yes, sparkling Champagne is made from the same grape varieties as Burgundy and yes, you can make white sparkling Champagne from black (pinot noir) grapes. The colour only comes from the skin: press the grapes gently and the juice won't be red it will be white. Well, greeny yellow actually.

I should also mention that those legal boundaries that have encircled the Champagne region have been allowed to be enlarged. Not of course to meet growing demand for celebratory fizz you understand, simply because the authorities in France have now decided that when the boundaries were originally drawn up, they were not quite right. There is one last thought that I will leave you with before I move away from Champagne and that is this: sparkling wine was first made in this region by accident. This region is so far north the grapes are on the margins of where you can get them to ripen; having enough sunshine is hit or miss and the wines can tend to be pretty acidic as a result. Champagne is allowed to legally have its flavour adjusted with the addition of sugar. The success of Champagne as a region has been to turn a marginal, still wine-making region of modest quality into the greatest region on earth for the making of sparkling wine.

I would add at this point that one of the most enjoyable and memorable bottles of wine which I have ever drunk was a bottle of Champagne. It was back in the 1990s and I ordered for a restaurant I was working at two bottles of Krug, which is about as good a Champagne as you will ever find. What should have been delivered was Krug Grand Cuvée but what arrived was something called Krug Special Cuvée. I had not heard of this and had never seen it and neither had the chef patron for whom I worked. We rang up the wine merchants and received an apology; the Krug Grand Cuvée was out of stock but they had two bottles of this that had been sitting in their cellars for some time and they hoped it would do. Well it must have been sitting in their cellars for a very long time because this particular Krug cuvée ceased production in the 1970s. That meant that the bottles must have fifteen or twenty years bottle age. Generally speaking Champagne, ordinary Champagne, is only aged for a few years before it is released onto the market. At around seven to ten years Champagne from specific vintages is usually at its peak. Great Champagne will age for longer but it starts to taste like something completely different.

The chef patron promptly gave me one bottle and took one for him. I opened mine some time later whilst standing outside on a mild spring evening. The aroma was so strong that I could smell the wine whilst holding the glass at waist height. The wine had gone a golden colour with age but it was still releasing a lovely, steady stream of tiny bubbles. It smelt like Champagne and Sauternes rolled into one: honey, nuts, oatmeal, it was divine and the taste matched the bouquet.

A couple of tips for buying Champagne: every bottle has a tiny code of letters and numbers on it. Those that start RM are basically wine from grapes grown and bottled by the same chap: a domaine in other words. Nowadays most Champagne because of supply and demand is released onto the market without as much bottle ageing as I think benefits the wines. So if you opt to buy a standard bottle of Veuve Clicquot, Pol Roger or Moet et Chandon for example, if you can ferret it away for 6 months or a year, it'll taste better.

What helps to assure the quality of Champagne as a product is that it is made with fine grape varieties and it is aged for a considerable time; or it should be, let us say. Notionally however, there is nothing to stop someone using chardonnay or pinot noir vines elsewhere and treating them in the same manner as the Champagne houses do and making something that to all intents and purposes tastes like Champagne.

Try Pelorus from New Zealand, Quartet from California or one of the sparkling wines now made in England such as Nyetimber.

Tarlant, which is one of my favourite Champagnes, I did not discover until 2006. This is a small family business that was established in 1687 at Oeuilly in the Marne valley. The vineyards they own are all well sited and the vines are generally fairly old; thirty years or more mostly. The wine making is meticulous and the vineyards are managed as naturally as is possible. By that, I mean they eschew the use of pesticides and chemical fertilisers which is a pleasant change from the norm – which which in Champagne seems to be an over-use of chemicals in the vineyard. The Champagnes are given a generous amount of time to mature and in blind tastings they score highly.

Delamotte, founded in 1760, is centred on the village of Le-Mesnil-Sur-Oger and they have fantastic vineyards of generally Grand Cru rank and mostly planted with chardonnay vines. Production is modest but the Champagne is very good across the whole range but do, if you can find some, try their vintage Champagne which is really what fine Champagne should taste like.

Drappier, at Urville, I first came across in the early 1980s and I was so taken with it I bought ten cases including some of the top cuvée, Grand Sendrée 1979 which was at the time the most impressive Champagne I had tasted to date with the exception of a Dom Perignon 1976.

Paul Déthune I first tried it in the late 1980s. This Champagne estate works organically and achieves richly flavoured wines of complexity from their own 7 hectare vineyard in the Montagne de Reims. This is a pinot noir dominated wine that I love. All of the vineyard is Grand Cru status; the Champagne is terrific.

Krug is an internationally famous name and many would argue is the greatest of all Champagnes. The style is distinctive, as is the bottle presentation. I was invited to a lunch for four guests back in the early 1990s which was arranged with Krug and one of their U.K. representatives. I can't remember much about what we ate but I can remember the wines pretty clearly. We kicked off with Krug Grande Cuvée. This is what you will invariably be offered if you go out to buy a bottle a bottle of Krug from a wine merchant or in a restaurant. The style of Krug is distinctive; owing mostly to the way the wine is made: the wine is oak barrel fermented whereas most Champagne is not and the wine is aged on its lees for around twice as long as most Champagnes. We were then served several vintages of Krug then the Le Clos du Mesnil which is single vineyard blanc de blancs vintage wine and finally a rosé. All were superlative.

The Loire Valley

The Loire Valley offers a wide range of wines all at really very sensible prices. If Champagne is as much a fashion statement as a drink then the Loire is at the other end of the spectrum. Here are wines to be drunk, enjoyed and integrated into daily living and they are all, by and large, priced sensibly and modestly.

Muscadet is rustic and refreshing at its most basic, but the best estates in good years make a white wine that, paired with seafood and especially shellfish, works really well. The best is usually labelled Sevre et Maine and if the label has the words "Sur Lie" on it the wine should taste a bit more complex too. Muscadet Sevre et Maine Sur Lie has missed out to all the New World inexpensive dry white wines which is a pity as, for its price, it is a pleasure to drink. It was the equivalent of New Zealand Sauvignon Blanc thirty years ago. Today it makes an excellent alternative, and there are a few dedicated growers who make wines that if you like crisp, dry, slightly flinty white wines you should give them a shot. **Domaine de 'Ecu** is one. Guy Bossard's vineyard is bio-dynamic (I will touch on this again later) and organic. His wines are intense and benefit from ageing, which is something that was not considered relevant for Muscadet in days gone by.

Muscadet lies at the western end of the Loire, Sancerre

and Pouilly Fumé are at the far eastern end. I'm jumping from one to the other because these three names are perhaps the best known of the Loire dry whites and although they are made from different grape varieties they share a vaguely common theme: they are crisp, dry white wines.

Sancerre and Pouilly Fumé have long had a following; they make brisk, dry white wine from the sauvignon blanc grape variety. It is usually un-oaked and was possibly the original inspiration for the New Zealand sauvignon blancs that burst upon the wine world and became so successful.

There are other communes near Sancerre and Pouilly that make similar wines but are less well known: Quincy has an older history of wine making and is good but the region is very small. Menetou-Salon is okay and so is Reuilly.

Sebastien Vaillant at La Cave de Valencay makes a sauvignon blanc with a generous splash of chardonnay thrown in which is as pungent as the local goats cheese, deliciously dry and brimming with rustic minerality. (There's some purple prose for you!) Valencay is a great alternative to Sancerre. The town has a couple of thousand inhabitants, a fancy chateau and it has a claim to fame as being the place where the first Special Operations Executive agent landed by parachute in 1941. There is a memorial there to mark this fact and commemorate the SOE's work during the Second World War.

Back in the early 1990s I assembled around twenty different Sancerre's for a restaurant to consider and then choose one to put on their highly acclaimed wine list. I tasted all the wines blind along with the owners of the restaurant and what struck me was the variation in quality from different growers all of whom had vineyards close to each other and gathered around one small village. The wine we choose then was made by a small domaine called Henri Bourgeois.

Henri Bourgeois has continued to build a good reputation and to acquire more land over the years and is now not just a major player in Sancerre but they have even bought a vineyard in Marlborough, New Zealand.

The key factors that can influence variation in wines from vineyards next door to each other are obviously how the vineyard is worked, when the grapes are harvested and how the wine is made. It is perfectly possible to have two vineyards side by side and for the wines to taste very different even if they are from the same grape variety.

For example, one vineyard might have vines that are closely planted together and were planted thirty years ago; these might be heavily pruned to reduce the amount of final bunches of grapes. The second vineyard may have been planted only ten years ago and the vine management might be more casual. The owner of the first vineyard might choose to wait until late in September to pick his grapes when they have reached their zenith of ripeness. The owner of the second vineyard however might have pre-booked his grape pickers for the last week in August and is unwilling to pay them to sit around and wait whilst the grapes soak up an extra week or two of sunshine. The owner of the first vineyard may be prepared to buy expensive new oak casks to age his wine whilst the owner of the second vineyard may be content to age his wine in concrete vats. The owner of the first vineyard might pay some skilled hands to pick over all of the bunches of grapes and remove any not fully ripe or mouldy prior to them being sent for fermentation. The owner of the second vineyard might not be fussed with such details.

So at the end of the day you may find two vineyards

next to each other and both will be labelled with the same name: whether that is Gevrey Chambertin or Coonawarra Cabernet Sauvignon yet they may well taste very different. The easiest way to appreciate this is to have some friends over for nibbles one evening and to buy three or four bottles of identical wines from different growers. This can be a fascinating and fun exercise and if you want to challenge yourself after you have tasted all four wines get someone to pour some wine from one bottle into a glass without you seeing which bottle it came from and see if you can identify it.

One last story on this subject. I was tasting wines one year at Pouilly Fumé and was with one grower who provided me with two wines to try. They were similar enough, but were nevertheless quite different. The first wine was acceptable; in fact I decided it was quite good. These next two glasses that he offered me were in another league; they were far better. Both tasted similar but not quite identical.

'Both from you I presume?'

'Oui, of course,' he smiled.

'Same vintage?'

'Certainly,' the winemaker smiled again.

'Different fermentation methods?' I suggested.

'Non.'

'Harvested at different times?' I ventured.

'Same time.'

The winemaker looked affably at me but with a twinkle in his eye. Come on then, he seemed to say, you want to buy my wine, well first you must pass this little quiz to show you know your onions.

'So the vines in the glass in my left hand are older?' I suggested.

'No, it is not the age of the vines; they are identical.'

'But are both of these wines from older vines?' I asked.
'Oui.'

I felt I was now making some headway.

French winemakers love to play such games. I have had dinner with a courtier (a chap who introduces wine makers to wine buyers for a small commission) in Burgundy and have been served half a dozen wines all decanted and was invited to comment to each.

Obviously in Burgundy only Burgundy is drunk and Bordeaux for example is eschewed. We were in the company of a couple of Burgundian winemakers. The first white wine tasted pretty good but was nothing sensational. Of course the challenge for us was to be brave enough to say that this wine was not very good and hope that it was not made by one of the gentlemen sat at the table! It was a white Burgundy from a great vineyard but from a dull year and was made by a grower who was not represented by the courtier but who did have a very high reputation. The next white wine was really impressive. The first red wine was pleasant, the next really fantastic and clearly also very old. After that came another. With every wine we were asked, just for fun, what we thought the wine was and what vintage we thought it might be.

The very last wine, served with strong cheese was another red. I was in the company of a British wine buyer and a wine merchant from London. We all sniffed our glasses, swilled our glasses and sipped from our glasses. I glanced sideways at whispered to my companion:

'It's a bloody Bordeaux!'

'Heck, you're right.'

Our host and his friends all thought this was great fun.

Petrol heads can close their eyes and hear a car and say that it's a certain type of Ferrari and who can't take a sip of tea with their eyes closed and know that it is Earl Grey or

Lapsang Souchong? There is no secret to blind tasting wine it is simply a matter of having a good memory and the opportunity to taste numerous wines.

Anyway, to wrap up the story at Pouilly Fumé I conceded defeat. The vigneron (winemaker) led me from the cellars and we walked across the courtyard and stood looking down a gently sloping hillside covered with vines.

'You see the rosebush at the end of the row of vines in the middle?'

'Yes,'

'The glass in your left hand is the wine I make with the vines to left of that bush and the glass in your right hand is the wine I make with the vines to the right of that bush. It was my grandfather who understood the difference. It is in nothing that you can see.'

I glanced sideways at him, squinting in the sun. He looked at the soil under his fingernails then pointed.

'The soil on the surface is all the same, the soil underneath is all the same but underneath that - there must be a difference. That is where the difference comes from.'

'How old are the vines?' I asked.

He shrugged.

'They were planted by my grandfather when he took over from his father and that was before the war. That field over there though, my father planted that is making good wine now. I have bought more land over the other side,' he waived vaguely, 'and planted vines seven years ago and the grapes are okay but you know…' he shrugged.

'So these vines here must be fifty or sixty years old at least?' I ventured.

'Oui. Every year they give me less grapes but every year, if the sun is good and the flowering is good and the wind is gentle and the rabbits keep away then I get better wine every year.'

'The vine roots must be very deep now.'

'Absolutment,' he nodded with satisfaction. I suddenly sensed that all of this was leading up to the price that he was going to ask for his wine when I would say that I would like to buy some.

Vine roots given time can go as deep as twenty feet or even deeper. The strata of soil, rocks and mineral-rich ground they are delving into can add to the nuances in the wine. Older vines yield less fruit but undeniably better fruit. That is why you will find French wine makers love to write "Vielles Vignes" (old vines) on their wine labels and even New World winemakers will proudly inform you on the bottle's back label that the wine might come from twenty or thirty of fifty year old vines. After around fifty years vines become so unproductive, that is to say they yield so few grapes, that it makes sense, sadly, to dig them up and start afresh. Nevertheless wines can be found that are made from really old vines and they are invariably gorgeous.

It is usual when tasting wines in situ to simply sip, spit and then tip what is left in your wine glass to the ground. Even if you are tasting in a wine cellar this is the norm and thankfully there is usually a drain to hand. If there isn't then the cellar floor will do. Now however, standing in the afternoon sunshine with a glass of wine in my hand that I knew was from such old vines, it felt wrong to simply discard what remained in the glasses. I could almost feel the grandfather looking down at me. I could imagine him planting the vines back in the 1930's. I drank what was left in both glasses and risked a last throw of the dice.

'The left glass is my preference,' I said.

The vigneron smiled benevolently and nodded in agreement.

'So tell me, how much a case for the wine from the old vines?'

'Oh monsieur, it is all already sold. But perhaps if you would like to buy some of my other wine then next year…'

Whilst talking about Pouilly Fumé, if you would like an exercise in subtle differences buy a couple of bottles of Sancerre and a couple of bottles of Pouilly Fumé and see the difference between these two neighbouring communes.

You'll also probably find as you explore wine that over the years your preferences will change. You will also find in time that you will encounter wines that should be great but are bitterly disappointing. When faced with a wine of high status with a price tag to match, it is not easy to taste it and immediately say with total conviction that it is disappointing because one tends to think that the wine must be good and that somehow oneself, the taster, is at fault, or perhaps "just not getting it." I once poured a bottle of Pouilly Fumé from the legendary wine-maker Didier Dagueneau. I was expecting something amazing and had opted to share this bottle with my parents and knew there would never be any more coming from Dagueneau since he had sadly died in a plane crash. My mother, a stalwart fan of sauvignon blanc and especially the wines of Sancerre and Pouilly, had been primed as to how amazing the wine was going to taste but even whilst I was still desperately trying to get something from the wine to match my expectation, she put her cards on the table announcing; "Maybe it's me but I don't get much bouquet or even taste from this wine." She was absolutely right but it took me five more minutes to come to realisation that the wine was a bitter disappointment. Maybe it was too old? Perhaps it was too young? Whatever it was though, it was not for me, as memorable as I had expected it would be. Wine is like that: occasionally a great bottle disappoints and sometimes a modest bottle of something unknown makes you sit up and take note.

Vouvray in the middle Loire has a very long history of making really serious bone dry white wines and some quite sweet, really complex wines too. Depending on the vintage conditions each year growers have opted for different styles but finding what I would call real Vouvray, rather than commercial Vouvray, is a challenge, and the difference is like chalk and cheese. The wine is made from the chenin blanc grape and my first experience of this grape variety was a basic chenin blanc from South Africa back in the 1970s. It was about as exciting as a glass of Robinson's Barley Water. My chenin blanc journey has now come full circle as I have recently had the pleasure of tasting some single vineyard chenin blanc from some serious wine producers in South Africa focused on quality not quantity, and the minerality, richness of flavour and complexity is just amazing.

Today chenin blanc remains in the second division, and that is a pity, but it is also a blessing. It is a pity because chenin blanc certainly makes some very good wine, but they are a tad unusual, a bit esoteric and they don't shout their wares. I had stupidly assumed that all Vouvray was dull after tasting just a handful ages ago and it wasn't until I tried the wines of Bertier Pichot that I realised that Vouvray could be really good and the good ones were not at all like those indifferent ones.

Bertier Pichot whose wines I shipped in the late 1980s, were made in small quantities from old vines, and, depending on the harvest date and how the wine turned out, might be pleasingly medium or off-dry or more likely bone dry with a high acidity and a palate, when approached young, that made them taste very un-friendly. However these wines developed with age, but with more age being needed than I ever imagined a dry white wine required.

When I stayed in Vouvray at Alain Jorand's home, who was a director of Bertier Pichot, he gave me the opportunity to taste old bottles which were intensely rich, mineral and full-bodied, but, had I just looked at the vintage on the label, I'd have expected the wines to be over the hill. Alain's house incidentally, like many in Vouvray, was partly built into a hillside and was a remarkable cross between house and troglodyte cave.

'I was born in 1938 and I can still enjoy a bottle from that vintage to mark my birthday each year,' Alain told me.

Huet and ***Clos Naudin*** are first rate producers of Vouvray and ***Marc Bedif*** is good too. Near Vouvray is a not dissimilar commune called Montlouis. The good news is that for wine drinkers who are less fashion conscious but recognise something interesting and worthwhile, chenin blanc, when well made, can offer really interesting wine at a really fair price. To make a risky sweeping generalisation: buy the most expensive chenin blanc that you can find - and it shouldn't cost all that much - it should be really good. Cheap chenin blanc remains something to avoid.

Savannières is a name to consider as another source of serious chenin blanc from this stretch of the Loire.

There is an ancient walled vineyard that was first planted in the 12th century that has the most perfect of situations to allow chenin blanc grapes to work to their full potential; the combination of soil type, exposure to the sun and degree of slope is ideal and the vineyard ***Coulée de Serrant*** makes arguably truly great wine, but it is not to everyone's taste. The wines made here by Nicolas Joly are, shall we say, distinctive.

Joly had planned to have a career in finance and went to Columbia University but things didn't go as planned and he came home and got involved with his family vineyard.

He then went on to embrace biodynamic wine-making after stumbling upon a copy of Rudolf Steiner's work on the subject and after adopting bio-dynamic practices he saw a dramatic turnaround in the quality of grapes and wine coming from the vineyard. At this point in time, very early 1980s, he was probably the first person to be making wine in France and perhaps in the World using bio-dynamic practices. He told others and the word has spread.

Bio-dynamic wine-making is something that I have to be honest about and say that I am really struggling to understand how it works in respect to it being different to organic wine making. The founder of bio-dynamic wine–making is Steiner (1861-1925) and he wrote dozens of works and could variously be described a philosopher, humanitarian and social reformer. I am trying to read his work "Theosophy" at the moment; it was published in 1904 and translated into English in 1922 and after reading the first 92 pages I have to say that I am completely baffled.

That said Steiner's recommendations have been taken on board now by numerous wine-makers who assert that they have seen a dramatic improvement in their wine as a result. At a most simple level I guess what he was saying was that the soil with which farmers were working in the 1920's was damaged by over user of fertilizers and pesticides and that the soil was becoming infertile. Bio-dynamic wine-makers adopt organic practices but they go to another stage with various preparations of natural ingredients which are put into the oil to encourage natural regeneration. The trouble with bio-dynamics is there is a fine line between explaining something and it sounding like sensible, well-founded practice and with it sliding on the other hand into the realms of mumbo-jumbo and witchcraft. That said I've spent a bit of time with Olivier Zind-

Humbrecht and what I can say is (a) he seems pretty normal and sensible and (b) he undoubtedly makes some of the finest wines in Alsace (if not some of the most perfect white wines in the World) and he works to bio-dynamic principles. I have tasted dozens of bio-dynamic wines and they have all tasted really good and it is therefore very difficult to dismiss or ridicule practices which may sound a bit odd when the final results taste so convincing. A footnote I might add is that personal research has convinced me that if one has a heavy night of drinking biodynamic (or possibly also organic) wines, the following morning I don't wake up with a splitting headache, which makes me wonder whether the traditional hangover is exasperated by not just alcohol but by the chemical gunk that goes into commercial wine.

The following are a few of the now many bio-dynamic wine-makers whose wines I have tasted and can say are good if not excellent:

In Burgundy: Leroy, Leflaive, Lafon, Trapet, Drouhin, Pierre Morey and Domaine Romanée Conti. In Alsace: Bott Geyl and Zind Humbrecht and Marcel Deiss. Huet in the Loire. Charpoutier and Eric Saurel in the Rhone, Chateau Falfas in Bordeaux and Domaine St Nicholas on the Loire.

There's loads of others whom I'm afraid I have forgotten but the areas where bio-dynamic wine-makers seems to be grouped are: Burgundy, the Loire, Alsace, Rhone, Oregon, Australia, Piedmont, Central Otago and Fruili Venezia Giulia but I'm sure I've overlooked other areas and for that I apologise.

To continue our journey along the Loire...

Late harvested, super ripe chenin blanc can make a very long-lived white wine that has a rich sweetness that suggests a dessert wine but has a balancing acidity and tautness that makes it altogether fascinating.

Coteaux de Layon is the bigger area that makes such wines but the best names on a label to search out are Quarts de Chaume and Bonnezeaux. These are classified as Grand Cru vineyards and have been highly regarded by those in the know for ages. They take time to develop and have a lot of complexity. A bonus is that they don't command high prices.

It is worth mentioning that there are also some really good wines, I mean really good wines, made from the chenin blanc grape variety that are grown in South Africa and Australia to name but two other places.

Raats Family Vineyard Old Vine Chenin Blanc from South Africa has a massive mineral nose and a long, full finish that makes it a wine to savour. This is one of the best chenin blanc wines that I have tasted. Raats do a less expensive chenin too but pay the extra and go for the Old Vine Family Vineyard if you can find it. I met Bruwer Raats recently and something he said struck in my mind. Now, try to read the bit in speech marks with a Boer accent and picture a stocky, broad shouldered guy looking you straight in the eye as he talks to you. "You know, all we grow is two grapes; chenin and cabernet franc. There are plenty of people who want to grow a bit of everything and try a bit of this and that and make a load of different wines in different styles and follow whatever is fashion. I can't be doing with that: I just grow chenin, I make chenin and I just try to make the best chenin. That is all I care about."

For reference the second grape variety that Bruwer Raats uses is cabernet franc; the wine is full bodied, seductively perfumed, distinctive and noteworthy.

The more general term for wines from the central Loire Valley is Touraine for the eastern bit and Anjou-Saumur for the western bit. Basic Touraine sauvignon blanc is roughly half as good as Sancerre and is roughly half the price. You can also get pretty good rosé and red wine from here too.

Chinon, Bourgeuil and Saumur Champigny make red wine from the cabernet franc grape variety. These can be okay in average years, good in good years and better than good in years when Mother Nature is truly kind. These vineyards are about as far north as you can expect black grapes to ripen fully, although curiously, they are well south of Champagne which grows a lot of pinot noir and meunier.

Chateau de Hureau in Saumur Champigny is worth trying.

I have tasted Saumur Champigny wines from half a dozen growers and have enjoyed them all and they aren't in the least bit expensive for what you get in your glass.

Domaine de la Cotellaraie in Saint Nicolas de Bourgeuil is very good.

There are some growers in South Africa who make wine predominately or exclusively from the cabernet franc grape variety.

Warwick Farm bottled a pure cabernet franc in the late 1980s which I tasted and was impressed by. This estate has built a notable reputation. More recently I have enjoyed a cabernet franc from **Raats** vineyard. I reckon that this wine will develop with more bottle age so I must remember to stash away a few bottles under the stairs.

The Rhone Valley

The Rhone runs from the centre of southern France, in pretty much a straight line down to the Mediterranean coast. The area is divided into a southern half and a northern half. The southern half is climatically undeniably hot but the mistral wind which is funnelled down the valley can help too cool things down a bit. The summers are though very hot indeed. The vineyards here were first planted by the Romans and this is mostly red wine territory. Stylistically the wines from here can have a lot in common with other Mediterranean wines like those made in Spain or Italy. There are numerous grape varieties, some famous, some not.

The area named Chateauneuf de Pape is the regional

star; these wines have been famous since the Middle Ages. The area was the first wine making region in France to be formally controlled and legally defined as such according to French law. Every wine book will tell you that there are thirteen permitted grape varieties used in making Chateauneuf du Pape but I have only ever knowingly tasted one wine made from all thirteen. Most growers content themselves with half a dozen at most. The most important grape varieties the production of Chateauneuf du Pape and indeed generally throughout the vineyards of the southern Rhone valley are syrah, mourvèdre, grenache, cinsault and carignan. All these grape varieties are grown elsewhere. In Spain grenache is called garnacha and in Australia syrah is called shiraz.

Other wine-making villages in the southern Rhone that are worth looking out for include Vacqueyras and Gigondas for serious wines and Luberon, Costières de Nimes, Rasteau and Luberon for good but slightly less hefty reds. Beaume de Venises makes both a fairly full bodied red wine and from muscat grapes a sweet dessert wine. I have always enjoyed the wines of the southern Rhone and spending a bit more often pays dividends. The best wines are never too expensive. The other day I tasted two wines both made by the same grower, **Clos de Caveau at Vacqueras.** Both were a blend of grenache and syrah, a "Fruit Sauvage" was an uncomplicated and satisfying wine; quite full bodied, very fruity but with some nice tannin and acidity to balance it. Nothing flash but thoroughly enjoyable. The other labelled "Carmin Brilliant" had two years more bottle age was altogether more noteworthy. It was just what I'd expect from this commune which knocks out wines that are not unlike the more famous Chateauneuf du Pape but cost less. Vacqueras and Gigondas have never disappointed me and some bottles are terrific, if you like a wine which is more rustic than refined. They can have lots of bouquet, rosemary and pepper, plenty of tannin and body. They're robust wines from grapes that have been drenched in Mediterranean sunshine. Forget elegance and subtlety, these are hearty wines for casseroles and game.

In the northern Rhone valley there are far less acres under vine but there are some first rate wines made, most notable are Hermitage and Cote Rotie. What the northern Rhone lacks in quantity it certainly makes up in quality. Hermitage and Cote Rotie are steeped in history and commanded high prices centuries ago for their famous wines. Standing looking at the vineyards you can see why they should make great wine. Steeply terraced vineyards that enjoy maximum exposure to the sun with poor rocky soil, they are ideally suited to fine wine making. Surprisingly the wines nowadays are not outrageously priced. In fact, I'd almost venture to say that in comparison with top Bordeaux, they are a bargain. This is all the more surprising because the vineyards are so small; the whole commune of Cote Rotie is smaller than some single properties in Bordeaux.

These wines are made from the syrah grape variety and they are big and powerful yet elegant and poised at the same time. They are for me winter-time reds to savour with roast deer and mallard like their counter-parts from the southern Rhone. However they have more complexity, more bouquet or should I say a more alluring bouquet? All the other communes in the area are worth exploring: Cornas, St Joseph, Crozes Hermitage are all satisfying. A more basic taster of what this region is about might be found under the label Cotes du Rhone Villages or Vin de Pays des Collines des Rhodaniennes.

Syrah wines can be also found elsewhere in southern France, as well as the USA, Australia and Chile. There will be wines from other countries too made from the syrah grape variety but for me these are the first countries outside of France that spring to mind. In Australia the syrah grape variety is generally called shiraz. Australian shiraz can range from basic and cheap to very good. Probably the best cue here is the price tag. There are growers in California who have championed the syrah but the wines have never caught on big time and many syrah vineyards were pulled up and replanted with other grape varieties. Chile is worth checking out and if you're prepared to pay twice the price of an average supermarket Chilean wine, I suspect you'll get something three of four times as good.

Vin de Pays is a category of wines according to the French wine system, France for many years classified all of their vineyards and created a four tier system of evaluation. There is a brigade of French Government-paid wine inspectors who bicycle around the country dutifully tasting every wine every year making sure everything is correct and making sure that every vineyard is planted with legally permitted grape varieties. Each region is allowed to make up to a maximum amount of wine each harvest to make sure that wines are not thinned and there are stipulations about what level of alcohol the wine needs to contain and so forth. It is a commendable system of quality control, if not without its faults, and of course whilst a few unscrupulous winemakers might still sneak through loopholes when no-one is looking, the system generally works pretty well.

The best wines of France were labelled A.C.(appellation controlée = a wine region with high standards and specific rules which wine makers must adhere to) then next rank down were labelled VDQS (vin de pays de qualité superiore = wines from countryside with more relaxed wine legislation). The rank below that was

"Vins de Pays" (wine from the countryside without much legislation affecting its quality and produce) and then the most basic was "Vin de Table" (wine fit for a table made from pretty well any grape variety and harvested from anywhere and not subject to any quality control of note). Germany, Italy, Spain all have created their own not dissimilar systems. Then along came the E.U and some chaps in Brussels decided that a new standardised system was needed that every country had to abide by. You can imagine what most wine-makers thought of that!

I might mention at this point that there have always been rule breakers and when they do it and the results are bad they are condemned but when the results are great they become a national hero rather like Robin Hood. It is easy to end up typing the word hero when you might have as easily typed the word heretic. Before I talk about wine heretics, let me finish the subject of the northern Rhone. They make an interesting and rare, dry white wine up from the viognier grape in a commune called Condrieu. Hermitage makes a little white too which is similar. There is also one single property called Chateau Grillet that makes a white wine and it was once so highly regarded that it received its own special appellation or legal classification. Alas now Chateau Grillet is not the stupendous wine that people once thought it was. I've not tasted it but the word from those who have isn't exactly stunning. But, if you fancy trying a white wine that is very different; something that is almost perfumed and makes you expect it to be sweet but is in fact dry but softly so... then try a bottle of viognier. The northern Rhone makes some under labels such as Crozes Hermitage Blanc or Condrieu but you can also find from elsewhere if you are prepared to search.

Some Rhone Valley wines that I like are:

Charpoutier whose vineyards have been bio-dynamic since the mid 1990s and whose wines under the direction of Michel Charpoutier (the seventh generation of this family to make wine) have become even finer than before and they have always been good as far as I was concerned. A Hermitage 1977 which was a light vintage still came second at a tasting of Rhone wines I held in 1987.

E Guigal are by Rhone standards large scale winemakers but they are really good too. Their single vineyard Cote Rotie wines are excellent. My tasting notes for their Cote Brune et Blonde have included prunes, blackberries, cedar, satin and spice and high scores.

Chateau de Beaucastel is one of the top names of Chateauneuf de Pape. I've tasted numerous vintages. Their reputation is top notch and I like the wine but think it a tad pricey.

Domaine Les Cailloux belonging to André Brunel is rich and concentrated and as good to my mind as any Chateauneuf to be found. Confusingly there is another Caillou, owned by the Vacheron family, Le Clos de Caillou and it's good too.

Domaine des Escaravailles is off the beaten track in Rasteau and is a vineyard at altitude and with age: sixty year old vines and accomplished wine-making by oenologist Philipe Cambie turns out elegant wine, velvety yet spicy and at quite modest prices.

Montirius estate owned by Eric and Christine Saurel makes both Vacqueryas and Gigondas to bio-dynamic methods and I've tasted numerous vintages of both wines and found them consistently good, never stunning but modestly priced for what you get.

What strikes about the wines from the Rhone, looking back through all my tasting notes is that whilst few wines have been sensational, the majority have been enjoyable and hardly any have been disappointing. I can't say the same of Burgundy, as much as I am fan of the wines, when they're good.

Wine Heretics

It used to be that a bottle of table wine cost a little, a bottle of Vins de Pays cost a little bit more, a bottle of VDQS cost somewhat more and a bottle of A.C. wine from France cost perhaps three or four times the price of any of the former.

It was like that in Italy and Spain and everywhere else where vineyards were mapped, graded and regulated and the governments had kept a watchful eye over what was going on and they had done so for as long as anyone could remember.

Then back in 1973 down in a sleepy viticultural backwater in the far south of France a chap called Eloi Durrbach bought a domaine and set about making wine using cabernet sauvignon and syrah grape varieties. Old books showed that these varieties had once been grown in this region and he was convinced that he could make great wine with these grape varieties although everyone else in the region used other grape varieties. The region was not noted for making anything other than ordinary wine. Durrbach was about to change that and during the 1980s a few people started to taste Trevallon and to take note. I first tasted it in 1986. It was then as good as other wines at twice the price.

In 1993 in an attempt to tighten standards the French

authorities issued new rules on what grape varieties could be used to make which wines. Their motives were doubtlessly well intentioned: it was to protect the historic local identities of regions and to discourage people from planting cabernet sauvignon and chardonnay willy-nilly in preference to local grape varieties. In the 1990s these two grape varieties had become internationally popular and everyone was getting on the chardonnay and cabernet sauvignon band wagon.

Domaine de Trevallon declined not to toe the party line and refused to dig up their cabernet sauvignon vines. A wine that was clearly A.C. quality was, as a result, demoted to Vins de Pays status simply because they were using too much cabernet sauvignon in their wine.

Durrbach continued; his wine was uncompromisingly well made and tasted like no other; he had striking labels that were different from everyone else's but he dutifully noted on the label that his wine was merely Vins de Pays. However instead of packaging his wine in cardboard boxes like everyone else in the region he boxed it in wooden crates as if it might have been from the top Chateaux of Bordeaux.

The quality of his wine and its stand-alone style marked it out for attention. The wine is now on the wine lists of most top Michelin starred restaurants across France, it has an international reputation and the wine is sold out from one vintage to the next before it is even made.

Domaine de Trevallon was perhaps one of the early estates in the south of France to signal what could be achieved. Everyone, I think the French included, believed that the best wines of France came from Bordeaux and Burgundy and the Rhone came in close behind them. The south of the country was regarded as an area that could make wine in volume and it could be good enough, but it was never seriously considered as a fine wine making region. Trevallon and others have proved that fine wines can be made in the far south of France.

The Far South of France

There are now a handful of wine makers down in the far south of France who have found well sited vineyards and they have set about producing low yields of good grapes rather than high yields of okay grapes. By following a perfectionist path from planting the vineyard to harvesting and fermenting the wine, then perhaps even lavishing some money on new oak casks, they are making really good wine and sometimes great wine from a region that yesterday had been considered as good enough but nothing exceptional. If you fancy searching out a few wine estates from the south of France that are perhaps a little bit off the beaten track but well worth drinking here are some that I have enjoyed:

Domaine Richeaume in Provence. This vineyard was started by a German in 1972 with just 5 acres of vines. Hennig Hoesch was an earlier pioneer of organic wine; the vineyard is grenache, syrah and cabernet sauvignon. I first tried this wine in the late 1980s. The domaine has grown in size and Hennig's son is now driving it forward.

Chateau Vignelaure in Provence. Whilst there was a Roman vineyard on this site it was after the 1960's that Vignelaure took off when Georges Brunet planted cabernet sauvignon vines here.

Mas Brugière in Pic Saint Loup. Planted in the 1970s the first vintage to be sold was 1986. Half a dozen different grape varieties are used and white is made as well as numerous different batches or cuvée of red.

Hegarty Chamans in Minervois. Significant investment since 2002 by the estate's new (English) owner has paid dividends and having a professional Burgundian winemaker on hand helps too.

Bandol is a modestly sized commune down on the Mediterranean coast. The Phoenicians planted vineyards here two and a half thousand years ago. The Romans shipped local wine out of the little port here two thousand years ago. It's safe to say that Bandol wines have been appreciated for some time. Most Bandol is red but some is rosé and both are good. The red is mostly mourvèdre and must by law be aged for at least eighteen months in oak. It is historically a big wine with great character and a generous level of alcohol. If you have watched the film "A Good Year" you may recall a reference made to the wine by Albert Finney.

Domaine Tempier. Lucien Peyraud worked hard to build this estate and generally to help preserve and then raise the reputation of Bandol. He was responsible for securing some appellation contrôlée specifics for the Bandol region during the Second World War and he ran the estate until he passed away in 1998. His heirs continue his good work. The vineyards are in a spectacular setting high in the hills looking down to the Mediterranean. There are four reds made each with a disconcertingly similar label but each rather different and all worth trying. The "Classique" sees mourvèdre blended with Grenache, cinsault and a drop of carignan and can be drunk from around five years old.

"La Migoua" is from vines grown on an elevation around 800 feet above sea level on chalk and clay over rocks that are 200 million years old. "La Tourtine" has a high proportion of mourvèdre and "Cabassaou" which is made in the smallest quantities has the highest proportion of mourvèdre of the lot at around 95%. Give the wine ten or fifteen years to mature. Enjoy with your closest friends drunk with a garlic clove spiked leg of lamb soaked overnight in olive oil, salt and thyme then roasted over a wood fire or finished on a BBQ with lots of rosemary.

Chateau Montus in Madiran is a great example of what a tannat grape variety dominated wine can taste like. As the grape name implies tannat can be very tannic: hard, chewy and potentially daunting. However when given time to age and made with care the tannat wines of Madiran region are great and can perhaps be considered as Gascon Claret but perhaps the wine-makers in both places won't agree with that! Montus is owned by Alain Brumont. He also owns Chateau Boucassé. Alain now has over 650 acres of vines so he is a major player in Madiran; He is also a major player because he makes really good wine and has done a lot to raise awareness of Madiran outside of the area. I first met him at a wine tasting in London; he was pouring his own wines for people at the tasting as and when they wandered off piste from the Burgundy and Bordeaux tasting tables. This was decades ago when he was less well known and when I hadn't even heard of Madiran. I had no idea what I was tasting when he poured me a glass of Chateau Montus. It was an awesome experience. Montus is best with a decade or so of bottle age; decanted and drunk with something like duck.

One of the work horse grape varieties of southern France is carignan but it's not a variety that has exactly blazed a trail to fame. I recently had an opportunity to meet Dan Odfjell Jr, whose ***Orzada 2011 Cargignan*** has been one of the most memorable wines that I have tasted in the last year. However this fabulous carignan is made not in southern France but in Chile. Having tasted other wines from the Odfjell stables, all of which were really good I got to talking with Dan for some time and he kindly offered to pen a few words about the wines for this book. I think what he's written provides a good window onto the world of bio-dynamic wine-making. The attitude and passion that so often seems to come with this way of making wine, really comes through. My thanks to him for taking the time to provide a fascinating insight into his wine-making.

Odfjell Vineyards
by Dan Odfjell Jr.

As I mentioned to you in Edinburgh, my passion for the organic and biodynamic principles was seriously awakened in October 2010. This was after not being at the winery for three years for personal reasons. I walked around our Padre Hurtado vineyards not knowing too much about what they had started working on (I knew about the organic project, but had not seen it in detail). What struck me immediately was how much life and vitality there was. I could feel something different was happening compared to earlier years. So the next day Arturo Labbe, our viticulturist who has been in charge of the vineyards since 1996, took me for an inspection in the morning. I asked him what had changed and he had a huge grin on his face. "You have never seen the biodynamic work we have introduced..." he said.

The more he talked, the more enthusiastic I became. Making our compost from a combination of left over grapes/stems, hay, horse and cow manure and biodynamic preparations. Creating our islands of biodiversity spread throughout the vineyards was something I never have heard about before. We also created biological corridors to attract insects from the hills surrounding the vineyards who act as natural enemies to the pests in the vineyards. So over the last couple of years, the more I learned and saw with my own eyes, the more I become convinced that returning to the "old" way of doing things is and should be the "new" way of doing things.

A Little History

My brother, Laurence, who designed and built our winery, told me that "the whole concept of our gravitational winery is to be friendlier to the grapes and their surroundings, which determines the way we work. This led us to the careful and detailed work in the vineyards and eventually to the organic and biodynamic farming methods."

Following the winemaking in Maipo, we decided to look for new terroirs in order to enlarge our portfolio of memorable wines, thus adding vineyards in Colchagua, Lontué and Cauquenes.

"The Orzada line of wines was born in 2001. Back then we went out to explore Chile in the search of grapes to complement the work we were doing at our Padre Hurtado vineyard. The wine that resulted was well above what we were producing for Armador, so we decided to create a new line to present this work."

Odfjell's specialty is the Carignan, and it comes from Tres Esquinas, our vineyard in Cauquenes, which we discovered in 2001 during our exploration of Chile. The Carignan grapes are from over 100 year old goblet-trained vines. The vineyard has no irrigation and very low yields, thus ensuring a perfect combination of concentrated fruit and complexity for our wines.

We saw great potential in these century old vines that have been worked by people from the same area for generation upon generation. It's a vineyard with tightly planted vines and for this reason the little mechanical work we do is done by our Norwegian fjord horses."

The Malbec variety is also one of our most renowned and highly awarded wines. Situated on the banks of the Claro River, the vineyard was planted in the 1960's. Its soils lack fertility and are worked entirely by horses. The Malbec grapes obtained from this vineyard are the key ingredient for our high-end premium wines.

Arnaud Hereu, our winemaker since 1997, born in Bordeaux, told me more about what terroir means to him... "The importance of terroir for me is when the grapes reflect the whole combination of vineyards, people, animals, climate and the way all these elements are managed together.

Arnaud further says, "In our vineyards we are organic and biodynamic so we are there looking for a complete expression of terroir. To achieve a truly sustainable biodynamic viticulture you have to take extreme care of everything. In the winery we try not to be invasive and enhance the fruit. We work with a careful selection and gravitational management, preserving what we receive from the vineyards. Our wines are also fermented in small lots between 800kg and 4,000kg, with pigage, which permits a delicate and optimal extraction process."

To emphasize how we focus on being different and unique, I quote Arnaud again, "I remember back in 2001 we were tasting with our then consultant Paul Hobbs and we didn't know what to do with the amazing new wines; we could mix them together to create a great blend or work to have various Gran Reserva wines focusing on each varietal. We called Laurence Odfjell and he asked "What is the easiest thing to do?" "Make one blend of all the wines", we answered. He answered "... then make separate varietals of each". This reflects the spirit and innovation of Odfjell. Orzada is like our DNA, always experimenting, exploring, searching for memorable wines."

As of 2013 vintage onwards all of Odfjell's vineyards are now managed and certified 100% organic and biodynamic. Laurence's comment was, "This is a great achievement for the winery and is the result of work over many years. It is a step farther in the owners' wishes since the origins of the company to make its wines something special, with personality, unique and unrepeatable; that the wine speaks of us, of the land, of the vine, of our people, of our project".

Arturo comment on same was, "The Demeter certification for Odfjell could be said to be a natural evolution of our manner of working. Since the beginning, in the 1990s with the first vineyards, the form of management was always to respect the environment, until the time came when we asked ourselves why don't we formalize this and certify ourselves organic. New motivations led us to biodynamic practices, which also made us decide to be certified, to give validity to our work"

Challenge for the future

Laurence told me that "Chile needs wines with character and searching for them is something we must do. There are good wines all over the world. Capturing and maintaining the attention of consumers is more and more difficult. Our challenge is to capture the imagination of consumers and maintain it in the future, delivering something that they won't find in any supermarket."

The Quest for the Perfect Vineyard

What has been learnt about making fine wine over the last few decades could fill a book but one of the key aspects of fine wine making that is now on everyone's lips is "cool climate". It is now taken as read that too much sunshine and heat can actually reduce the quality of wine dramatically. Everyone has gone in search of cooler climates; whether it is wine growers in Chile moving away from the valley basins and heading into the foothills of the Andes or wineries in Australia looking to get out of the sun, everyone is searching for the vineyard setting where the sun shines for as many hours a day as possible but it doesn't shine too fiercely.

Peter Althaus from Switzerland went on this quest and after looking at possible sites in many places around the globe he settled on the Coal River Valley in southern Tasmania. A couple of years ago a friend of mine went on holiday to Tasmania and he hasn't been back since. He raves about the countryside which reminds him a little bit of his native Scotland and he tells me that I have to get out there and try the wines as they are really good.

Well, I first tried Tasmanian wine back in the early 1990s when Andrew Pirie's wines came on the scene. They were noteworthy but since then until recently I have not explored Tasmanian wines any further. Meeting Peter Althaus and having the chance to listen to him and then taste his wines I feel certain that he has correctly spotted one of the best possible places to make fine wine.

Domaine A is cabernet sauvignon focused with merlot, cabernet franc and petit verdot in supporting roles. He does also make a very small amount of pinot noir. The vineyard enjoys a cool climate, very long sunlight hours and is planted on 200 million year old Jurassic Dolerite. I tasted five of Peter's wines ranging in price from what I might expect to pay for a good pinot noir up to three times that for his Domaine A Cabernet Sauvignon 2005.

The Stoney Vineyards Cabernet Sauvignon 2007, my preference of the wines I tasted, had a massive and expanding bouquet that changed from eycalyptus and mint to truffle as it opened and an elegant and long finish on the palate. At six years old it was drinking perfectly well but I'd like to re-taste it at twelve years old. The "Petit a" is twice the price. Maybe there's too much merlot (30%) in it for my palate or perhaps the 2008 is too young but I'd prefer to drink the Stoney Vineyard. The Cabernet Sauvignon 2005 is Peter's top wine; even more expensive and excellent. It strikes me as a serious wine that will repay cellaring for some time.

A pattern I see emerging amongst so many of the fine wines that I like is that the wine-makers behind these wines are not constructing wines to a recipe but rather they seem to let the majority of the work happen in the vineyard. Andrew Gunn, proprietor to Iona Vineyard in South Africa, expresses this quite neatly in the following brief chapter which he kindly penned for me.

Freshness and Purity
by Andrew Gunn

"Great wines require freshness and purity of fruit which can only come from the vineyard, assuming the vines have been planted in the appropriate climatic conditions. At Iona we have cooler average temperatures than Burgundy in January and February (July and August in the Northern Hemisphere) with temperatures marginally higher in March when the Pinot Noir is picked and moving higher in April when the last of our Sauvignon Blanc is picked. These optimum conditions allow us to ripen both varieties reliably with wonderful natural acidity and low pH. Whenever I congratulate our winemaker, Werner Muller on another great vintage, he humbly says, "Andrew, I am merely the custodian of the fruit, it all happens in the vineyard!"

Alsace

The region of Alsace lies in eastern France close against the border with Germany and the wines have some similarities to their neighbours but retain a distinctively individual style. The vineyards stretch north to south for around a hundred miles and lie in the foothills of the Vosges Mountains. The climate is very good for making wine and indeed for making fine wine. The majority of wine made here is white and the main grape varieties are riesling, pinor gris, muscat and gewürztraminer. Pinot blanc, sylvaner, pinot noir and other varieties are also used and a little pinot noir is grown to from which rosé and red wine is made.

The vineyards here were established by the Roman legions and by the Middle Ages the region was famous for its wines. Sadly wars between France and Germany and the region lying close to the border have seen the vineyards suffer.

Alsace lies in the lee of the Vosgnes Mountains; rainfall is modest, spring time is generally warm, the summers sunny and the autumn dry and long. Combined with vineyards of volcanic soils of granite, gneiss, schist and more besides, this region offers a fine wine making environment.

The white wines of Alsace are often highly aromatic and quite full bodied. They echo the white wines of

Germany just across the border but whilst the German wines frequently for me seem more delicate their Alsace counterparts are more robust and often better suited to drink with food rather than savour on their own. To me it remains a mystery why today they are so often overlooked. The wines are fairly modestly priced despite the limited production: Alsace produces under half the volume of wine that Burgundy does and under a quarter of the volume of Bordeaux.

Alsace pinot gris shares the same grape variety as Italian pinot grigio. Italian pinot grigio can range from dull to good depending on the grower. Alsace pinot gris however can range from good to truly stunning depending on the grower.

The region has a handful of co-operatives all with solid reputations and the cave de Ribeauville whose wines I first tried in the 1980s have consistently made good, modestly priced wines and provide a good introduction to what this region offers.

There are a lot of organic and bio-dynamic wine makers in Alsace. The classification system for Alsace is pleasurably straightforward. Aside from a little sparkling wine (cremant d'Alsace) the wines are either Alsace or Alsace Grand Cru. There are fifty-one vineyards that drop into the latter category. The grape variety that is a wine is made from is invariably prominently displayed on the label and varieties are very seldom mixed together.

Hugel and *Trimbach* wines are both excellent and not too hard to find.

Bott-Geyl and *Rémy Gresser* are harder to find with small quantities of super wines.

A bottle of Hugel Vendange Tardive Gewurztraminer

1976 I drank in 1988 was amongst the most memorable wines I drank that decade. This wine is made from late harvested super-ripe grapes from a prime vineyard area. The natural alcohol level can potentially go up to 17 or 18 degrees so the final wine fermenting out at around 13 degrees is left brimming with natural sweetness which is then counterbalanced by the wine's acidity. These fine Alsace wines have an ability to age for a decade or two effortlessly. The 76 which I drank in 88 tasted fabulously fresh and whilst for some mad reason I drank it with chicken Kiev the wine was so richly flavoured it overwhelmed the garlic butter soaked chicken effortlessly.

In 2008 I hosted a tutored wine tasting for some American guests who were visiting Scotland and whilst they were familiar fans of top flight Napa chardonnays and the best wines of Burgundy it was a bottle of wine from Alsace and not a familiar chardonnay that stunned them.

Zind Humbrecht Clos St Urbain Rangen de Thann Pinot Gris is for me one of my favourite white wines.

It is difficult to not fall in love with this wine; the experience is perhaps a little like being used to appreciate the great medieval cathedrals of Europe and then to be shown Gaudi's La Sagrada Familia. One point to keep in mind though is getting your hands on a bottle. The wine is made in very small quantities.

It is curious though that rarity does not always amongst great wines push the price into the stratosphere whilst some fine wines made in fairly generous quantities are for some reason excessively highly priced.

Chateau Latour from Bordeaux sells for around five times the prices of a bottle of Grand Cru Charmes Chambertin for example and yet the whole of the Charmes Chambertin appellation is roughly one tenth of the size of the Latour estate.

What's the Candle For?

"What's the candle for?" is a question I am often asked when decanting a bottle of red wine. The candle is simply a light source, held underneath the neck of the bottle so the wine in the bottle is illuminated sufficiently for you to be able to spot the sediment as it slides up the bottle whilst you gently pour the wine into a decanter. A candle looks special, romantic, mystical perhaps but a torch with a couple of new batteries would do a far better job.

Lots of good red wines throw sediment and decanting wine a way of separating the clean wine from the sediment that lies in the bottom of the bottle. It is also a simple way of getting some air to the wine and if it is a young wine this may help it to taste more appealing. Some powerful red wines can also taste better if they are exposed to air. Conversely some wines which are old and frail will only get worse when exposed to air. People invariably think about red wines when decanting red wines but some white wines can also benefit from decanting because they need to breathe.

I hosted a wine-tasting for a dozen guests once which was focused on Bordeaux and we tasted ten wines. One of the ten was a 1967 Chateau Lafite Rothschild. It is always interesting to see what a great wine can achieve in a bad year. The Lafite showed a beautiful bouquet as I poured some into my glass and made my initial comments. However in the time that it took to pour twelve tasting glasses of the wine and to pass them to everyone the wine faded markedly and whilst the handful of people who got to taste it first could appreciate the bouquet those who were served last were served too late.

There is still debate about whether decanting is a good thing or a bad thing or whether it is necessary or not. Being able to separate the wine from the sediment seems to me like a good idea. I always decant my red wines unless I think that they will not throw a sediment and that they won't benefit from breathing. Wine is about personal taste, so if decanting lights your candle, then do it. There is something quite pleasant about taking time to decant wine and decanters are lovely to look at, so I am all in favour.

Considerations about when to decant pale into insignificance though when put up against the consideration of when should a certain bottle of wine be drunk? When is a certain vintage from a certain estate at its best? Of course there are plenty of books with vintage reports and tasting notes and now the internet seems to provide a vast repository of information about particular wines and what they taste like and when they should be drunk.

All well and good but keep this in mind: we all have only our own palates and whilst someone may consider a certain wine is perfect now, someone else may be adamant that it should not be drunk for perhaps another two years. As you get to find the style of wine that you like best, you will be the best placed person to decide whether you are happy with a wine when you drink it. But the best way to appreciate the conundrum of when to drink any wine can be demonstrated thus: buy yourself four bottles of a wine you want that the back label or your friendly local wine merchants says needs to be kept for let us say five to eight years. Try a bottle after three years and another bottle every following two years, keep notes and then look back to see which you liked the most.

There are other rewarding and enlightening options: one is having found a wine that you like buy a couple of bottles and put them to one side. Then buy a subsequent vintage of the wine once it becomes available, drink one or two and keep one of two of these. Do the same with another subsequent vintage. Then have a few good friends for some drinks and a bite to eat and offer up three different vintages of the same wine. A second is to choose a theme for an evening; perhaps a particular year and invite your friends to bring a bottle from that particular vintage. Have all the bottles wrapped with brown paper so that their labels (and neck foils) are concealed, then serve the wines during dinner and simply invite people to comment on how much they like each wine. Last time I did this I had one friend who was a red Burgundy fan go head over heels for a wine that turned out to be from Oregon.

An Onerous Task

'Are you sure you know your way?'

'Of course,' I answered with emphatic confidence.

I waited until the there was a gap in the oncoming traffic then swung a right. If I could find my way around Bordeaux, Burgundy, the Rhone Valley, the Loire Valley and elsewhere, navigating from the wrong side of the road for a right hand drive car and managing to get to all of my vineyard appointments on time, then I could surely get to a famous five star hotel on Park Lane, London.

'I'm sure that sign said "No access except for taxis and buses", which we went past.'

'I think you will find that it said "No access for taxis and buses", unless I am very much mistaken,' I answered.

We were walking up a sweeping flight of stairs and I was admiring the fact that the brass banister was gleaming and free from handprints. Maybe everyone just used the lift?

'What about that sign that said "One Way Only"?' asked the other junior sommelier who I had brought along.

'Well, we were only going one way,' the other laughed.

'There was no such sign,' I pointed to our left, 'It's in here.'

A handful of men in city suits milled about at the doorway and behind a desk a smartly dressed young lady in a crisp white blouse and grey jacket was making sure that everyone who entered the room signed a visitor's book.

The white clothed tables stretched down either side of the hall as far as the eye could see and the bottles of wine were lined up like ammunition in a fort under siege.

I don't want to generalise or stereotype but I always feel I can glance around a trade wine tasting and quickly identify who is who or at least who does what. I signed in, gestured to my two colleagues to do the same and then glanced around.

Lots of city suits; a few with loud red braces which were then fashionable for certain people. There was a young chap with black jeans and a corduroy jacket who was moving up one side of the room, picking perhaps one wine in six, quickly swilling, sniffing and then discarding the wine without so much as a sip. If I'd been a cowboy and had walked into a saloon then I'd have singled him out the gun slinger to be reckoned with. The room was large and there already quite a few people present but everyone was talking seriously in hushed tones. Serious business this, tasting wines; you might have thought this gathering were politicians trying to thrash out a solution to a regional conflict, so serious was the atmosphere.

There was a middle aged woman, brightly dressed in contrast to the men in grey and navy who surrounded her. I recognised her as a notable wine personality. Another woman I spotted, who had a first class spitting technique, was almost already three quarters of the way around the tasting. I guessed she must have arrived very early; perhaps she'd even breakfasted at the hotel? I thought we had done well to arrive just an hour after the start time, given the drive that we'd had. The woman was rattling through the wines at a formidable speed, making scribbled notes after every wine.

There was an elderly chap in a tweed suit complete with fob watch chain, polka dotted silk handkerchief and fountain pen. I watched him for a moment. He would stand and pour himself about a third of a glass of wine, then scrutinise the label and then look at his tasting sheet. He then snorted the wine, took a mouthful, worked it like mouthwash for a good few seconds then holding one hand thrust out in front of him to keep people from his path he marched across to a spittoon and spat out the contents, carefully holding his tasting notes to his chest whilst the wine arced ahead of him and splashed against the metal side of the spittoon.

He then discarded the wine left in his glass, chewed thoughtfully and gave the impression he had some corn on the cob stuck between his teeth. Finally he would go and sit back down and take up his fountain pen and write a few sentences. I watched him move from wine number five to wine number six and reckoned that to tackle all the wines thus would take him three or four days.

'What's the plan then?' asked one of my junior sommeliers.

I glanced at the tasting schedule. It was formidable and there was nothing mediocre on offer. The wine merchants staging the tasting did not do mediocre.

'We do all the white Burgundies first then we do all of the New World chardonnays which will be an interesting comparison and then we stop for lunch. After lunch we taste the red Burgundies first, the red Bordeaux after them and the red Rhone last of all.'

'They've got Stag's Leap Vineyards from three vintages!' chimed one of my junior sommeliers.

'Crickey,' I glanced at the New World section more carefully, 'Well maybe we do the Rutherford Bench in between the Bordeaux and the Rhone.'

'Is the Rutherford Bench where we sit and have a break?'

'Very funny. Come on let's get started.'

I had not even poured myself the first of the white Burgundies when the first distraction came into my path. A pleasant distraction that I decided was far more worthy of my attention than a mere Puligny Montrachet.

'Mark, how nice to see you; how're things?'

'Tara, hi. I'm fine. How are you?'

I was acutely aware of the eyes of my two junior sommerliers upon me as I made small talk with Tara. In fact I was acutely aware of their eyes feasting on Tara; a brand agent for a Champagne House who had met with me several times to try to convince me to switch my choice of House Champagne to the Champagne that she represented. Whilst I talked with Tara my colleagues worked their way from the Puligny Montrachet and Chassagne Montrachet village wines to the Premier Cru wines, then some Meursaults and on to the Grand Cru Montrachets that were on offer.

Montrachet is a single vineyard of Grand Cru status which the villages either side, Puligny and Chassagne have hyphenated to their own name such is its value. Next to the vineyard of Montrachet are Batard Montrachet, Chevalier Montrachet, Bienvenues Batard Montrachet and Criots Batard Montrachet which are also Grand Cru vineyards. All these vineyards are tiny; Montrachet is about 20 acres and the eighteen or so owners who have parcels of land here I reckon are sitting on some of the most expensive land on the planet, which is odd when you think that it is just a slope of a field with some vines in it. Nevertheless the last time a parcel of vines were sold they went for half a million euros. Criots Batard Montrachet is probably smaller than a croquet lawn.

I swirled the Puligny Montrachet in my glass and tried to regard it objectively as I continued to chat with Tara. The Puligny Montrachet, I noted, showed good legs and the bouquet was as enticing as the flavour satisfying. To use a common wine term; the Puligny was "showing well". I glanced at the label to memorise the grower's name: Jacques Prieur. As I jotted down my tasting notes on the wine I caught a faint whiff of Tara's perfume as she leant towards me.

'What do you think?' she asked conspiratorially.

'Very good,' I nodded affirmatively as I jotted some thoughts on the tasting sheet I held.

It was not a wine that was easy to spit out and the flavours were many and mouth filling and even after swallowing or spitting, the taste lingered. I'd noticed this with great wines; the taste stayed in the mouth long after I had swallowed the wine.

I was left to focus my attention on the Puligny Montrachet from Leflaive and escape Tara's gentle pressure for me to buy the Champagne she represented. The Leflaive wine was good and was just one of an array of their wines on offer. It wasn't cheap; in fact there are plenty of Puligny Montrachet wines from other growers which are less expensive but Leflaive make first rate wines and the old maxim "you get what you pay for" held true for their wines at least.

My job as wine buyer for a five star hotel with a Michelin starred restaurant meant that I had to manage a cellar and wine list that matched the exactingly high standards set by the Head Chef who directed the kitchen where a dozen chefs slaved over a hot stove for never less than twelve hours a day. What made my job all the more exciting was that the hotel, although a fine Palladian mansion built in the 19th century, was newly created and still in its infancy, so the cellar I had taken over needed to be developed. By cellar I don't mean the physical cellar but I mean the collection of wines within it.

My brief on joining the hotel, which employed around a hundred staff, was succinct: I had to achieve a certain level of profit and I had to create a wine list that matched the best in the country and won critical acclaim for its breadth and depth. In other words a wine list was needed that included a roll call of all of the great wines of the world from all the best vintages, as well as a list that included something from every wine producing country that there was and from every significant region. I had a budget to achieve this and it was part of my brief that I had to go to every wine tasting possible in order to buy whatever was necessary to build this mega wine list. I also had to teach my junior sommeliers about the list and the wines on it so that they could, at the very least, have a basic knowledge of every wine on the list. There were already over three hundred wines on the list and I wanted to take this number up to five hundred as fast as I could, as I knew there were plenty of gaps on the list that I had inherited.

I was expected to have tasted all the wines on the list except perhaps for the rarest and oldest but these I needed to have researched so I knew what they were like. The list was pretty conservative but it matched the expectations of the day. I played safe, making sure for example that I listed wines from every single commune of Burgundy and Bordeaux and had a spread of vintages which were great, good or at least above average. I was though already of a mind to throw in a few unusual wines which I had come across and I liked such as a Jasnieres. I had to be careful though; the managing director when I served him the Jasnieres was not impressed one bit.

'What is this Mark?' he held his glass at arm's length

as if it contained something that might be poisonous.

'Jasnieres, it's made from old chenin blanc vines.'

'Really?'

The way he said "really" made me realise that next time he was dining I had better serve him a white Burgundy or I would be getting my P.45. I duly took note but it was not the last time I was to ruffle his feathers.

Jasnieres is a very small and historic wine making area on a tributary of the Loire. The soil is flint and tuffeau; the wines have intense minerality.

'Mark, why have we switched our House Champagne to something no-one has heard of?'

'Because it is better,' I replied.

'Than what we have?'

'Yes.'

'I had an invitation to a Pol Roger luncheon; what about Pol Roger as a House Champagne?'

'I have considered Pol Roger; I've actually looked at half a dozen possible well known Grand Marque Champagnes as possible House Champagnes but I feel that what I have chosen tastes better. Would you like to try it?'

'Well yes, I think I better had.'

I sensed I had perhaps taken my free hand a little too far by switching the House Champagne to my preferred choice; no-one knew the name, myself included, up until the day that I had tried it. I had bought it from a relative new wine merchant, a bit of a one man band, and had declined offers from numerous other agents for the big Champagne Houses. One had offered me a visit to Champagne, flights and accommodation paid, another had given me a case full of samples to try and of course perhaps most tempting of all there was Tara who seemed to hint that her thanks to me for choosing her Champagne would be a reward that I knew I really wanted and deserved.

I knew that if I simply served the hotel's managing director with a glass of the Champagne that I had chosen as an aperitif before his next dinner I was doomed; he would feign indifference. I therefore sent an invitation to him, the General Manager, the Front of House Manager, the Head of Sales and Marketing, the Banqueting Manager and the Head Chef to a Champagne tasting in one of the private dining rooms on a Wednesday morning. I chose a Wednesday morning because I worked out that this was the day when everyone was least stressed.

First through the door at 11am was John who was the Banqueting Manager. John was a hard-working, ever cheerful bon vivant who was good at sales, good with people and liked by all the staff. This made him unpopular with Front of House Manager who reminded me of Mr Todd: that fox in a waistcoat character from Beatrix Potter who was impossibly charming but not to be trusted. John though, however good he was at his job, never looked as smart or as calm as the Front of House Manager who was impossibly charming to every lady he met and frostily aloof to every chap he met, who for whatever reason ruffled his feathers.

Alan the Head Chef arrived at the same time as the Melissa, Head of Sales and Marketing who was a steely woman who worked from an office converted from a guest bedroom that, it had been decided, was actually too small to sell at as the hefty rates the hotel charged. She had two staff working for her who were young and talked as if they had plums in their mouths and these three were seldom seen by any of the other staff. Alan was polite, to the point and didn't suffer fools. He seemed to like me because I showed a genuine interest in his food and in the afternoons when he was in his office and the kitchen was calm I would always stick my head around the door with any samples of prospective new wines that I had received for him to try. In exchange he made sure I got to try anything he reckoned I should know about.

The General Manager and the Managing Director arrived together still discussing targets and figures as they walked in.

'How long will this take?' the Managing Director glanced at the table I had set out with a couple of dozen glasses and six Champagne bottles all already opened with the neck foils removed and the bottles wrapped in pages from yesterday's Financial Times.

'Ten minutes,' said John, quickly picking up the first bottle and pouring a small amount into glasses which he handed around. Like me he knew the M.D. kept to a tight schedule.

'As you may know, I've chosen a new House Champagne based on quality and price but I think it would be good to see whether it is of a style that goes down well or whether we can find something else that is preferable,' I said as matter-of-factly as I could.

Everyone held a glass and the silence was palpable. I had written a number one to six on a sticky label on each bottle and given everyone a tasting sheet so they could at least score each wine even if they couldn't be bothered to write any comments.

Alan the Head Chef had dealt with all six wines before John and I had got to number four and the others were still trailing behind us.

'I think number two is complete crap; number three isn't even Champagne but it's okay I suppose. Number six it the best, number five is the second best. I've got to go.'

Alan gave me a nod of encouragement and then he was gone. The rest of the gathering finished all the wines in stony silence.

'Well, what do you think Melissa?' the Managing Director turned the spotlight on the Head of Sales and Marketing.

'I scored number six with a ten. I think it's best.'

'What scores did you give the others?' I asked.

'I gave number five an eight out of ten, the others were all okay but those two are the ones I like.'

I gave a silent "Yes!" to her statement as the Champagne that I had put my neck on the block for was number five and number six was a great Champagne for sure but way too expensive to ever be a House Champagne. Without knowing it both Melissa and Alan had given me endorsing votes of confidence.

The Managing Director continued by asking the others their opinions without giving away what he thought. The only person he did not consult was me. As each person gave their views I watched him jotting stuff down on his tasting sheet. He was obviously not Managing Director just because he was older than the rest of us.

'Well done Mark,' he said at last, 'I should say that number five is perhaps the best choice for us as a House Champagne.'

'Why not number six?' John asked with a wry smile.

'Because it is most likely twice the price,' the Managing Director looked to me to confirm what he had said.

'Yep, you are absolutely right sir, number six is nearly twice the price of number five which is indeed my choice of House Champagne.'

'Good, well done Mark,' the Managing Director nodded as if satisfied, glanced at his watch and with a curt thank you to everyone for attending he left. As soon as the door was closed I sensed everyone relax fractionally.

'That was very interesting, thank you Mark,' the General Manager offered me a hand shake and then he too left.

Now everyone else visibly relaxed. Melissa folded her tasting notes into three and then slid it into the inside pocket of her jacket. She then poured herself a glass of number six.

'He's still not happy that you dropped the House Champagne that we had, you know that don't you?' Melissa said.

'But this is so much better.'

'Mark,' John put a hand on my shoulder; 'The Champagne House that you have dumped in preference for your unknown new one had put a lot of effort into getting this account.'

'However,' said foxy Front of House Manager, sliding his Mont Blanc back into his Saville Row jacket, 'this is far superior to what we had before, which on reflection I think is really rather common now, don't you?

I suspected this was a trap so I hesitated and instead poured myself a top up of number five.

'Our lord and master plays it safe but you know...' foxy held his glass up to the chandelier and admired the colour, 'I think Michelin might be impressed if we listed Mark's choice as our pouring Champagne. Don't you think so too John?'

John glanced at his watch, took another sip and then put his glass down.

'Must go, lovely to see you all. Cheerio chaps. Love the skirt Melissa.'

Sure enough within a week I was told that we would revert to our original House Champagne because they had now offered us a deal where, for every twenty cases we bought, we received a case for free in addition. So I had to be content with listing my new find and selling it when I could by the bottle whilst the Champagne that was poured by the glass and offered as our House Champagne remained the well-known Champagne name that was ubiquitous throughout the fine dining restaurants of the country. There was nothing wrong with it, but I thought it a shame that we had declined to have something better because it was less well known.

That, however, was not the end of the Champagne saga. Six months later the Managing Director came to dinner with his wife and two guests. As aperitifs, instead of asking for his usual glass of Champagne for himself and Kir Royale for his wife, I was called to the cocktail lounge. When I came into the room he stood up and shook hands with me and then introduced me to his two guests, a charming French couple. He then asked me to choose a bottle of Champagne for them to start the evening with.

'Nothing ordinary Mark. Whatever you like.'

I served them a bottle of the Champagne that I had been championing. As usual the wine choices to accompany the dinner were left in my hands. There was no question of serving anything other than French wines. I played it safe and uncorked a Puligny Montrachet and was then literally decanting a Chateau Palmer 1978 when foxy Front of House Manager found me.

'Is that for our lord and master?'

'Yes.'

'No good. They're from Saumur, you'd best serve something from the Loire. They've got a Chateau on the Loire that's a boutique hotel which has just joined the same marketing consortium as we're in. Have you got any Loire stuff that is decent?'

'But what about this?' I abandoned decanting the Chateau Palmer and almost banged the bottle down in irritation.

'Oh don't worry about that; we'll sell that tonight to someone else, just find something from the Loire that'll impress.'

'He hated the Jasnieres.'

'Well anything else.. surely there must be some decent wine made somewhere along the Loire I've driven it on holiday, its bloody long enough!'

So I duly served a Chateau de Tracy from Pouilly Fumé, then a red Sancerre from Domaine Crochet which being pure pinot noir I knew would make for a good alternative to a red Burgundy. With the dessert I poured glasses of Quarts de Chaume which I thought great but I was edgy that being chenin blanc my boss would not appreciate it.

'Good wine choices Mark, thank you.'

'Pleasure sir.'

'We all thought the Champagne was excellent; Monsieur Tallibet was telling me that it's actually the House Champagne at Maxims and the Orient Express.'

'Really sir?'

'You know Mark, I think that even if it costs a bit more we should consider it as our House Champagne.'

So the change of Champagne was made.

Jura

Jura is one of the least well known wine regions of France alongside Savoie. Jura is also a large island off the west coast of Scotland with thousands of deer, a few people and one distillery. The island immediately to the south of Jura is also large, more populated and has around eight distilleries the best of which are internationally famous and the island is called Islay. If Islay is to malt whisky, what Burgundy is to fine wine, then Jura is to malt whisky what Jura is to fine wine. If you see what I mean?

The grape varieties used in Jura are poulsard, trosseau and pinot noir for red wine and savagnin and chardonnay for white. In Savoie they use also mondeuse and gamay for red and altesse, chasselas, jacquère and roussane for white. If this has just introduced you to grape varieties that you have never heard of before, don't worry you're in good company.

I have not visited Jura or Savoie and have tasted precious few of these limited quantity and locally appreciated and consumed wines.

To give you a geographical bearing if you drive east from Burgundy towards Switzerland and stop half way between the two, very roughly you'll be in the right area. Savoie is close to the Alps and Geneva. I have tried Rousette de Savoie made from altesse grapes and enjoyed it. Stylistically this is miles from chardonnay or sauvignon blanc or anything else; I suspect altesse could become an internationally appreciated cool climate grape but meantime there are other varieties that are only just receiving a little of the due attention that they deserve.

There are numerous other smaller wine regions in France that are worth discovering and a few names worth hunting out would include:

Cotes du Vivarais – from the l'Ardeche; good reds; rich and full bodied but juicy with it.

Cahors – historically dark red wines made mostly from the malbec grape variety

Cassis – a small region on the south coast and not to be confused with crème de cassis.

Off the Beaten Track

I tried not to look down too much as the 4X4 swung around another bend on the dusty track and continued its climb upwards. On my left, dislodged stones from the edge of the track tumbled away into space. Far below I could see the house where we had met Alvaro an hour earlier. The little white building looked too small even to be a doll's house. To our right old vines, laden with grapes, covered the precipitous mountainside.

Alvaro pulled the 4X4 to a halt and we climbed out. I took another gulp from my bottle of mineral water, chilled when we'd set out it was now warm. The hillsides shimmered in the heat. The sky was cloudless, the sun bright and high. A bird of prey circling high above where the mountainside was just bare jagged rock caught our attention.

'An eagle; we have two pairs of eagles on the estate now and twenty-six different types of birds at last count. Before there was less wildlife but since I have reduced the amount of chemicals we use by ninety percent, we have enjoyed more wildlife. The garden we drove past used to be where they changed the oil on the tractors and it looked terrible. I cannot work in such a mess and I don't like to live that that; that hillside across there is how I like everything to be.'

I regarded the vineyard where Alvaro was pointing. The vines were terraced in neat rows and the sweep of vines was flanked by trees. I reckoned that this vineyard was the highest I had visited and the slopes were steeper than any I had seen planted with vines. It made sense that Alvaro's last trip abroad from Portugal for inspiration had been to Switzerland. Now, looking at the more recently planted slopes with carefully spaced, uniform rows of vines I could appreciate that Alvaro had brought some Swiss efficiency and common sense to the ancient vineyards of the Douro that he managed.

'This is hotter than normal for so late in the summer,' Alvaro confided. 'Look at these vines, in this part of the vineyard which is old, all the varieties of grapes are confused together. There was no system in the old days except for growing every variety and to hope that something would ripen well. This one here is touriga franc. This, taste this; this is tinta roriz.'

'They taste so different,' my girlfriend said, pulling grapes from under their canopy of broad leaves, 'this one is different too, isn't it?'

'Yes, that's touriga nacional. There are many different varieties. In the past everything used to be fermented together as well. Now we are systematic and I have planted the vineyard so we can harvest each variety when it is properly ripe.'

We took lunch back at a restored old farmhouse on the banks of the Douro. From the shade of the terrace we could sit and admire the river and the hillsides on the opposite bank, shimmering in the heat haze. Cold meats, cheeses, olives, little homemade crisps and a gorgeous, chilled white wine started the leisurely lunch. Tasting it blind I might have thought the wine an Albarino, a pinot gris perhaps from Alsace, maybe a Rousette de Savoie. It was very good and a little unusual and it turned out of course to be one of Alvaro's wines. Roast lamb with rosemary, diced and lightly fried potatoes, aubergine, green beans with garlic and a red wine followed. The red wine could have been a good Gigondas or perhaps a fine Australian shiraz/cabernet or something special from the Tuscan coast but of course it was another wine made from Alvaro. Finally we finished with a golden hued dessert wine. I wondered about it being a fine Mosel trockenbeerenauslese or a good Jurancon moelleux, but of course it was another wine made right here, in the Douro valley by Alvaro.

I had assumed until now that the Douro made great vintage port but nothing much else of note. Now I knew I was quite wrong. This meandering river valley had all the potential to produce fine wine in many styles, although I sensed the very best would be the big, yet elegant red wines that every restaurant in the region offered at a range of prices from modest upwards.

Lingering in Porto for a few days for a break we tried the local food and local wines in every good restaurant that we could find. Fine dining is not common here but there are a few very good restaurants.

Portugal is now seeing a trickle of top notch international wine-makers moving in and I shouldn't be surprised if that trickle turns into a torrent. The landscape and climate is ideally suited to make first rate wines with an emphasis on reds and whilst I hope that it is the local grape varieties that are given a chance to shine, I can see syrah being a runaway success here.

I should mention that the river Douro subtly changes its name on the Spanish side of the border but continues as a Spanish wine region of note: Ribera del Duero.

Spain and Portugal have in recent years seen a massive wine renaissance and hitherto unappreciated wine regions, once known just locally, have come to the attention of a wider audience.

Rias Baixas up in Galicia in the far north-west of Spain makes lovely, crisp, dry white wines for which its cool climate is ideal. I bought Albarino in the 1990s as a house wine for a restaurant and it was then unusual but now it is widely imported to the U.K and you can frequently find bottles in large supermarkets.

Somontano close to the Spanish border with France is another region for modestly priced, good, mid-range wines.

Toro is an area that must surely come to the attention of a wider audience? The local grape here is Tinta de Toro, fabulous old bush vines dotted across a barren stony landscape make ***Numanthia,*** a sensational wine, dark and brooding and lusciously perfumed.

Conca de Barbera, also in the north of Spain but further east is noteworthy.

Utiel Reqena to the west of Valencia has as a region upped its game from everyday wines to more stylish offerings from producers who are pursuing higher aspirations than merely headily alcoholic red wine to wash down rich, local food with.

La Pamelita is perhaps the most unusual of all New Wave Spanish wines that I have tried. It is a red, sparkling wine made from syrah grapes by a Scottish wine-maker, Pamela (Geddes) Lobban who trained in viticulture in Australia. I like it as an aperitif and also with chocolate desserts.

Manga del Brugo from Calatayud is made by Norrel Robertson a gifted Scottish Master of Wine and winemaker. It's really old vine garnacha with some syrah and tempranillo. I met Norrel in Edinburgh and tasted a range of wines he is making in this off the beaten track corner of Spain. He mostly works with old vine garnacha but he also makes a heady viognier. In his pursuit of making fine wine he has worked with some grape varieties that are not accepted by the local authorities and has had to make one wine out-with the regional classification it should have received; not altogether unsurprisingly he's named the wine ***"Dos Dedos de Frente"*** which I believe is a Spanish expression to suggest someone is being a little dim-witted.

The landscape and climate of Portugal varies dramatically from north to south and from the coast to inland.

Tras os Montes is Portugal's most north-easterly wine region. Vines are grown at altitudes of 350 to 700 metres above sea-level on mountainous granite and schistous terrain. Alcohol levels can be high but the wine can be balanced; the reds richly layered and the whites intensely aromatic.

The ***Douro***, famous for Port, is a region of great potential and the best reds are really good and still very reasonably priced. The region also makes whites wines and even sweet wines of high quality.

Tavora Varosa is to the south of the Douro; the vineyards are high and the region is cooler. The region has yet to make a name for itself internationally and I think this little region is a spot to watch.

Beira is a large region in central Portugal that runs alongside the Spanish border. Try a white from the local Fonte Cal grape variety: though you may struggle to find the wine outside of Portugal.

There's a wealth of wine producing regions around Lisbon; Colares is one of the oldest and most famous but this whole area is buzzing with new wine activity. Colares wines are made from the tiny ramisco grapes and the wine is austere when young but once the tannins soften, layers of flavours and revealled. The soil here is so sandy that the nasty phylloxera bug that wiped out nearly all the vineyards of Europe back in the 18th century was unable to survive in the soil here and as a result these are now some of the oldest un-grafted vines in Europe.

Dao and ***Bairrada*** are historic old regions that are on the brink of being revitalised. Julia Kemper in Dao is an estate to watch. Her white wine is excellent. I suspect that serious fine wine makers will move into these two regions and put them firmly on the fine wine map.

What really struck me after two visits to Portugal was the vast array of different grape varieties that there are. There are over two hundred and fifty and all are historic, indigenous varieties – your internationally grown varieties hardly get a look in. How often in Britain do we get to encounter a wine made from the Esgana Cão? It means, dog strangler, by the way. Some of the other varieties have equally curious names: lady's Finger, Long Foot and Donkey Loader, to name but a few.

In some areas wine-makers will blend numerous varieties together, and whilst this may not help with consumer branding the products, I believe it contributes to the rich and unusual flavours of these wines and presents a formidable array of styles. We maybe don't know the names of these grape varieties and they are certainly hard to pronounce but after visits to Portugal to explore what wines are on offer I am convinced that Portugal has fine wine making potential in abundance.

In Lisbon at the Club de Jornalistas over lunch one day, I mentioned that I was writing a book on wine and in no time at all the table at which my girlfriend and I were sat was filled with glasses, each being filled with different wines. Their hospitality knew no bounds and it was very late in the afternoon, or maybe it was very early in the evening, when we waved goodbye. I had scrawled as many tasting notes over the menu as I could and looking at it now it, it presents a confusing array of names, most of which were new to me. Flor do Tua DOC Tras-os-Montes, Viosinho, Codega de Larinho had beside it "rosemary and lemon" and whilst the wine was delicious, I doubt I'll ever find a bottle outside of Portugal.

'That was a very good lunch,' I said, looking up and down the cobbled street and trying to remember which way was the way we had come.

'What was your lobster with mango like?' my girlfriend asked.

'Lobster? Did I have the lobster, I thought I had octopus?'

'Mark, which way are you going?'

I turned around and pointed.

'We need to go the other way.'

'That's what I thought. You know, I'm sure I had octopus and it was with rosemary.'

'You did, to start and then you had lobster. Don't you remember?'

'I clearly remember they insisted that we tried an awful lot of wines.'

'All of which were very good.'

'Very good.'
'It was a very good dinner.'
'Lunch.'
'Was it lunch? Yes, it was a very good lunch.'
'What time is it?'
'No idea.'
'You were just looking at your watch.'

'Quite,' I scrutinised my watch again. 'Do we have a restaurant booked for dinner?'

'Yes, probably, I can't remember. What time is it now?'

'It's…' I looked at my watch again. 'Do you think it's normal in Portugal to spend so long over lunch? Hang on a minute… I've left my tasting notes behind!'

'I put them in my handbag, come on, let's go back to the hotel, I'm dying for a cup of tea.'

'Are you certain you've got my tasting notes?'
'Yes, I've got your tasting notes.'

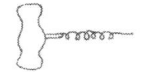

Printed in Great Britain
by Amazon